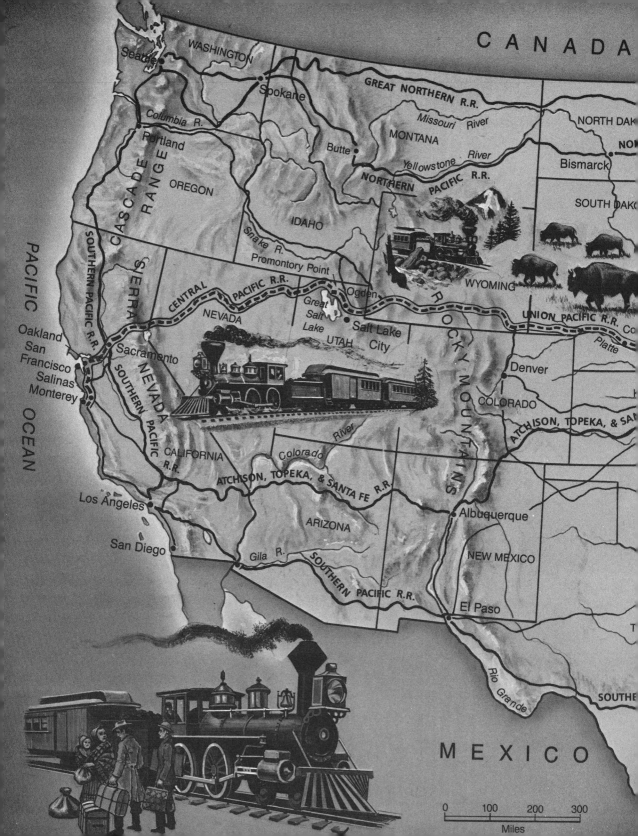

CANADA

WASHINGTON

Seattle

Spokane

Columbia R.

GREAT NORTHERN R.R.

Missouri River

MONTANA

Butte

Yellowstone River

NORTHERN PACIFIC R.R.

NORTH DAK

NO

Bismarck

SOUTH DAKO

Portland

OREGON

IDAHO

Snake R.

Promontory Point

CASCADE RANGE

SIERRA NEVADA

SOUTHERN PACIFIC R.R.

CENTRAL PACIFIC R.R.

NEVADA

Ogden

Great Salt Lake

Salt Lake City

UTAH

WYOMING

ROCKY MOUNTAINS

UNION PACIFIC R.R. Co

Platte

PACIFIC

Oakland

San Francisco

Salinas

Monterey

Sacramento

SOUTHERN PACIFIC

CALIFORNIA R.R.

Denver

COLORADO

ATCHISON, TOPEKA, & SAN

OCEAN

Los Angeles

San Diego

Colorado

River

ATCHISON, TOPEKA, & SANTA FE R.R.

ARIZONA

Gila R.

SOUTHERN PACIFIC R.R.

Albuquerque

NEW MEXICO

El Paso

T

Rio Grande

SOUTHE

MEXICO

0   100   200   300

Miles

Robert Louis Stevenson's route west in 1879 ▰▰▰▰

Map shows major railroads of the United States–1912

Across America
on an
Emigrant Train

ACROSS THE CONTINENT.
"WESTWARD THE COURSE OF EMPIRE TAKES ITS WAY."

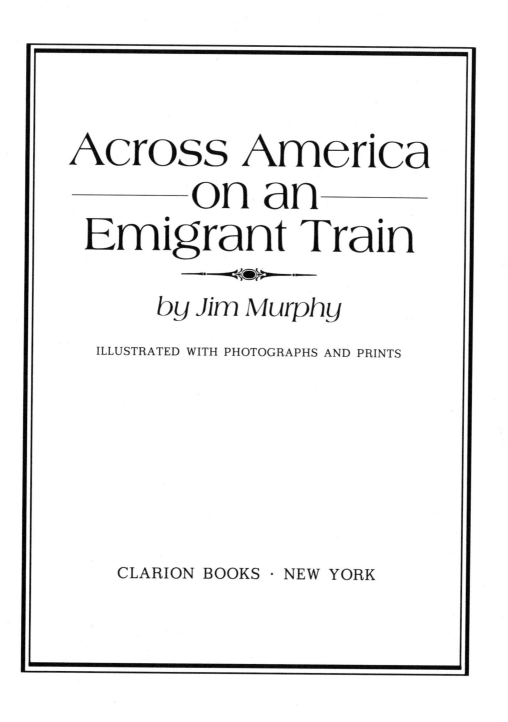

Across America
——on an——
Emigrant Train

by Jim Murphy

ILLUSTRATED WITH PHOTOGRAPHS AND PRINTS

CLARION BOOKS · NEW YORK

Clarion Books
a Houghton Mifflin Company imprint
215 Park Avenue South, New York, NY 10003
Printed in the U.S.A.
Endpaper map by George Buctel.
Drawing of Fanny Van de Grift Osbourne,
p. 134, by Chris K. Soentpiet.
Book design by Carol Goldenberg.
www.houghtonmifflinbooks.com

Library of Congress Cataloging-in-Publication Data
Murphy, Jim, 1947-
Across America on an emigrant train / by Jim Murphy.
p.   cm.
Includes bibliographical references and index.
Summary: Combines an account of Robert Louis Stevenson's experiences
as he traveled from New York to California by train in 1879 and a description
of the building and operation of railroads in nineteenth-century America.
ISBN 0-395-63390-7   PA ISBN 0-395-76483-1
1. Stevenson, Robert Louis, 1850-1894—Journeys—United States—Juvenile
literature. 2. United States—Description and travel—1865-1900—Juvenile
literature. 3. Railroad travel—United States—History—19th century—
Juvenile literature. 4. Authors, Scottish—19th century—Biography—Juvenile
literature. [1. Stevenson, Robert Louis, 1850-1894. 2. Railroads—History.
3. United States—Description and travel.] I. Title.
PR5495.M79   1993
828'.803—dc20   [B]   92-38650
CIP   AC

VB   10

Acknowledgments

It would have been impossible to do this book without the generous assistance of the following individuals and institutions: Joyce Koeneman, Association of American Railroads; Eddie DeFell, Atchison, Topeka and Santa Fe Railroad Company; Robert MacKimmie, California Historical Society; Blaine P. Lamb and his staff, California State Railroad Museum; the Chicago Historical Society; Patrick Fraker, Colorado Historical Society; Robert W. Richardson, Colorado Railroad Historical Foundation, Inc.; Stephen V. Melito, the DeGoyler Collection; Eleanor M. Gehres, Denver Public Library; Jenny Watts, the Huntington Library; Barbara Puorro Galasso, International Museum of Photography at George Eastman House; Christie K. Stanley, Kansas State Historical Society; the staff of the Library of Congress; Tracey Baker, Minnesota Historical Society; Leslie Nolan, Tony Pisani, and Marguerite Lavin, the Museum of the City of New York; Marty Miller, Nebraska State Historical Society; Laird Ogden and Diana Arecco, the New-York Historical Society; Marcia Eymann, the Oakland Museum; Benjamin F. G. Kline, Jr., Railroad Museum of Pennsylvania; Gayle Yiotis, the Smithsonian Institution; Stanleigh Bry, the Society of California Pioneers; Andy Kraushaar, the State Historical Society of Wisconsin; the staff of the Union Pacific Railroad Museum Collection; and John Lovett, University of Oklahoma Library.

*For Dorothy Briley, with appreciation
and thanks*

Contents

*People came to America for many different reasons. In a highly
unusual experiment, these wayward boys from the Earl of
Shaftesbury's Reform School in England were shipped to Wakefield,
Kansas. It was hoped that loving (but strict) foster parents and the
harsh agricultural life would make productive citizens of them.*
(Kansas State Historical Society)

Introduction

————◆————

THE UNITED STATES went through monumental changes
between 1850 and 1900. The Civil War was fought, putting
an end to slavery and forging the independent-minded states
into a powerful union. Settlers pushed westward. A transcontinental railroad was built to link the East to the West Coast,
opening the door to swifter travel. And a great wave of people
left their homelands overseas to start a new life in America. In
fact, the second half of the nineteenth century saw over sixteen
and a half million people settle in the United States, making
this one of the largest voluntary emigrations in the history of
the world.

There were many reasons for emigrating. Famine and eco-
nomic depression drove some people to seek a new beginning;
others were fleeing slavery or repressive governments. Still
others wanted to live where they could practice their religion
openly and without fear. Each person or family had a compel-
ling reason for leaving—but this does not account for why the
United States was such a magnet for them. In general, people
want some assurance that what they are traveling to is, in
some way, better (or at least not worse) than what they are

leaving behind. So why did so many choose the United States and not countries closer to home? The answer was a combination of genuine opportunities and freedom, shrewd business, and good advertising.

Early in the nineteenth century, the federal government of the United States began to realize just how vast and valuable the land west of the Mississippi River was. Millions of acres of timber stood waiting for the axe, endless stretches of fertile soil begged to be farmed, and minerals such as gold, silver, and copper were there to be mined. What's more, the West Coast was ideal for ports of trade with countries like Japan, China, India, and Russia. There was a problem, however: in order for these resources to be secured and exploited, large numbers of United States citizens had to be living on that land.

Several thousand people from the East Coast could be expected to migrate west every year, but more people were needed. Millions more. To get the necessary bodies, the government relaxed the already easy immigration laws and urged citizens to make the new arrivals feel welcome. This wasn't hard to do, once businessmen learned that these people brought in more than mere muscle power. A Congressional report in the early 1870s estimated that "every foreign labourer landing on our shores is economically valued at 1,500 dollars." The report went on to state that in less then ten years these people would add $4.8 billion to the wealth of the nation, a vast sum of money back then.

As immigration to the United States increased throughout the 1850s and 1860s, officials began to tackle another problem. To move these people to the West as quickly as possible, a system of transcontinental railroads had to be constructed. Naturally, building such railroads required a great deal of

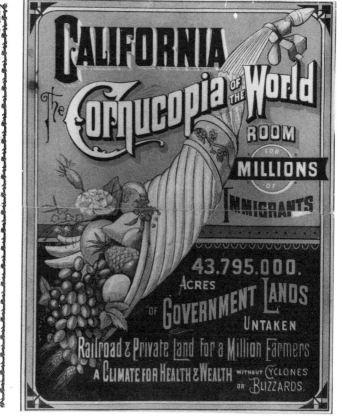

LEFT: *This German-language "Guide to Southern Minnesota and Eastern Dakota" describes a region which "has no equal for agriculture." For those interested, railroad land agent P. G. Peterson stamped his name and address on the cover.* (Minnesota Historical Society)

RIGHT: *Many western states vied with one another for the emigrants (and the cash they brought with them). Thousands of pamphlets like this one were handed out to new arrivals to the East Coast. What more could a person want!* (New-York Historical Society)

money. Track laid on flat land cost about fifteen thousand dollars per mile; in rougher mountain terrain, the costs skyrocketed to over fifty thousand dollars per mile. To encourage construction, the government gave the railroads 155,504,994 acres of land with the right to sell it for a profit. It did not seem to bother many people that all of this land was home to Native Americans.

In order to sell as much land as possible, railroads began competing for the emigrants. They flooded one European country after another with posters, pamphlets, and books promising religious and political freedom, low railroad-ticket prices, and cheap, fertile land. The truth was often stretched and sometimes completely ignored. "Sunshine cheers the settler nearly all year long," a booklet extolling the virtues of Kansas promised. "There are long, beautiful springs, short winters, and the fall is a perpetual paradise."

To reinforce this literature, hundreds of railroad pitchmen were sent to Europe and parts of Asia to persuade people to buy their land. The Burlington North Railroad Company had over eight hundred fifty agents going from country to country selling people on the virtues of life in the United States. These agents proved to be remarkably persuasive. One who worked for the Santa Fe Railroad, C. B. Schmidt, was so good at his job that he managed to get fifteen hundred Russian Mennonites to abandon their country in one great exodus.

Once the initial wave of emigrants had settled in, the settlers wrote to relatives and friends still living overseas. Life wasn't as easy as the pamphlets had promised, they would say, but life *was* better. And so new emigrants would follow the old, a pattern that continued for the rest of the century.

After several decades of emigration, the government had what it wanted—millions of citizens living and working in the

West. As for the railroads, they got buyers for their land, passengers for their trains, and, when the farmland began producing crops, customers for their freight cars. There was another, less mercenary result from this intense advertising campaign: in the eyes of millions of people around the world, the United States was firmly established as the land of freedom and opportunity.

Travel in the nineteenth century was always difficult and could be painful and dangerous. This was especially true for poor emigrants. At sea, they were often packed into the bowels of creaky freighters with no fresh air and poor sanitary conditions, and given the vilest of food. Those who traveled into the interior of the United States were crammed into ancient and uncomfortable railroad cars like so many head of cattle.

This book follows the trip of one such emigrant, Robert Louis Stevenson. Stevenson realized that his reason for going to America was unusual, so he always referred to himself as an "Amateur Emigrant." Still, he covered the same hard miles, endured the same discomforts and pain, and felt what just about every other emigrant must have felt along the way.

The words "emigrant" and "immigrant" are used in this book as Stevenson used them in his writings about his trip. To emigrate is to leave or depart from a country or place. To immigrate is to enter or arrive in a country or place. Stevenson's traveling companions, though they had entered America, had not yet arrived at their final destinations. He apparently considered them still in the process of emigrating.

Stevenson's story began on a summer day in 1879 when a messenger arrived at his door with an urgent cable from America.

Robert Louis Stevenson as he looked in 1879. At the time, his hair was thought to be daringly long and unruly, and his overall appearance was considered eccentric. (California Historical Society)

1

The Journey Begins

IT WAS SUMMERTIME 1879 when a brief cable from America reached Robert Louis Stevenson in Scotland. The exact words of the message have not survived, but Stevenson told a friend that "F. seems to be very ill," and that she had "brain fever."

The news upset Stevenson tremendously, and sent him into frenzied motion. It took only three days for him to pack two small bags, borrow around one hundred ten dollars from friends (this plus what he had came to just over two hundred dollars), and set off for the nearby seaport city of Glasgow. There, on the chilly morning of August 7, he boarded the steamer *Devonia* and began the ten-day journey to the United States.

Stevenson was a struggling twenty-nine-year-old writer at the time. In his journal he managed to capture the feeling on board as the ship left the busy harbor and slowly gained speed. "The sun was soon overclouded, the wind freshened and grew sharp . . . and with the falling temperature the gloom among the passengers increased. Any one who had come aboard might have [thought] we were all absconding from the law. There was scarce a word interchanged, and no common sentiment but that of cold united us. . . ."

In some ways, Stevenson *was* fleeing. He left Scotland without telling his parents, and gave his forwarding address to only one friend with strict orders that it be given "to *no one,* not even the Queen." The reason for his secrecy was simple: his parents and most of his friends did not approve of his attachment to the "F" referred to in the cable.

The woman who upset so many people and who inspired Stevenson's hasty departure was an American named Fanny Van de Grift Osbourne. Stevenson had met Fanny four years before while on vacation outside of Paris. At first, they had been just friends, having dinner together with mutual acquaintances and visiting local artists. Over the weeks and months that followed, a romance developed between them. For the first time in his life, Stevenson found himself deeply in love.

The fact that Fanny was an American was one reason his family and friends disapproved of her. Americans were considered coarse and common, not at all fit to associate with a respected Scottish family like the Stevensons. Another reason for shunning her was her age. Fanny was over ten years older than Stevenson. In the strait-laced society of Stevenson's time, men always courted and married women younger than themselves. Anything else was considered unseemly.

These two things were major obstacles to a relationship between Fanny and Stevenson, but could probably have been overcome with time. Another much more important fact stood in their path: Fanny was married and had two children.

It didn't matter that Fanny's husband spent most of his time wandering through the hills of Colorado, Montana, and Nevada searching for gold and silver, or that he often ran up huge debts and left Fanny to deal with them. Nor did it matter that he was distant and cold to Fanny during his brief stops at home. The circumstances of her marriage did not matter; all that mattered was that she was married, and for her and Stevenson to become romantically involved was looked upon as sinful.

Thomas Stevenson, Robert's father, was so upset by the situation that he tried to get a friend of his son's to break up the romance. "For God's sake use your influence," he wrote in an impassioned letter. "Is it fair that we should be half murdered by his conduct? I am unable to write more about this sinful mad business. . . . I see nothing but destruction to himself as well as to all of us."

Obviously, none of his family's objections swayed the younger Stevenson. As far as he was concerned, Fanny was perfect in every way. She was small and fine-boned, with a dark, mysterious complexion. An acquaintance of Stevenson's noted that her "eyes were full of . . . mystery as they changed from fire to fun to gloom or tenderness." Stevenson wasn't attracted to her simply because of her exotic looks. He admired her independent spirit, her keen mind, and her strong opinions. She could talk intelligently and with authority on a wide number of subjects, from art and politics to travel and literature.

Both extended their visits in France so they could be together, and Stevenson thought about asking Fanny to marry him. He did not propose, however, but not because of pressure from his parents. He hesitated because his meager income from writing was not enough to support her and her children comfortably. He hadn't yet written *The Strange Case of Dr. Jekyll and Mr. Hyde, Treasure Island,* and the other novels that would make him rich and famous. At this time, he had only two thin travel books to his credit, neither of which had sold very well.

The rough Atlantic Ocean tosses this steamer around, spraying the deck each time the ship plows into another wave. (Author's collection)

So Stevenson had held off proposing to Fanny, hoping a lucrative writing assignment would come along. Then one day Fanny received word that urgent family matters required her to return at once to her home in California. She and her children left a few weeks later, and a saddened Stevenson returned to Scotland alone. They exchanged letters for over a year. Then the telegram arrived, and Stevenson found himself rushing to her side.

The moment the Scottish coast was out of sight, the *Devonia* hit foul weather and rough seas. A strong headwind pounded the metal ship and forced the giant steam engines to rumble and hiss and belch oily black smoke as the vessel struggled to crash through the waves. Stevenson had not been able to afford to sail first class, but he had scraped together enough for a cabin in second-class steerage (which meant he did not have to sleep in the ship's hold with other poor passengers). During this first day out, Stevenson's stomach grew queasy with the constant tossing of the ship. The next morning, he woke up itching all over and discovered that his bedding was infested with lice.

The bad weather kept Stevenson cooped up in his cabin, where he spent his time scratching at the lice and writing in his journal. Yet he was never really alone, as this journal entry makes clear: "Through the thin partition [I could] hear the steerage passengers being sick, the rattle of tin dishes as they sat to meals, the varied accents in which they converse, and the crying of their children terrified by this new experience."

The only time he left his cabin was to have something to eat, though even this did not prove to be enjoyable. "We were served . . . some broken meat from the saloon . . . but as a general thing, [we were given] mere chicken-bones and flakes of fish neither hot nor cold. If these were not the scrapings of plates their looks belied them sorely; yet we were all too hungry to be proud and fell to these leavings greedily."

The bad weather—and Stevenson's seasickness—persisted for five long days. Then on the sixth day, the sky cleared and the seas calmed enough to allow for safe walking on deck. When he emerged, Stevenson breathed in clean, cool air that had a brisk, salty smell to it.

Other passengers began emerging from the ship's dark interior, and soon the deck swarmed with nearly sixty people. "The company was now complete, and began to draw together, by inscrutable magnetisms, upon the deck. There were Scots and Irish in plenty, a few English, a few Americans, a good handful of Scandinavians, a German or two, and one Russian; all now belonging . . . to one small iron country on the deep."

Stevenson was an eternally curious individual, particularly about the people around him, and he made it a point to talk with as many of his fellow passengers as possible. What he discovered surprised him. He had always assumed that most emigrants were much like himself—in their twenties and without the responsibility of providing for a family. He reasoned that a young, single person could afford to set off on a risky adventure and could best endure the physical hardships and dangers of the journey. His informal survey told him something altogether different.

Families made up the majority of the travelers—husbands and wives along with their small children. Many of the men were in their forties or older; there were even a few elderly grandparents in the group.

Their reasons for leaving their countries varied widely. Famine had forced many to flee, while others were escaping religious or political persecution. One man was so secretive about his past that Stevenson wondered whether he was wanted for

The deck is crowded and there's not much to do but read old letters, nap, or watch the rolling sea. This photo was taken on board the Patricia *in 1902, but the scene on the* Devonia *probably looked much like this when rain wasn't falling.* (Museum of the City of New York)

some ghastly crime. While a few had been successful in their homelands, a surprising number had been "unable to prevail against circumstances in the one land, [and] were now fleeing pitifully to another; and though one or two might still succeed, all had already failed." This sounds harsh, but, at the time, Stevenson considered himself a failure as a writer and was including himself in this statement.

No matter what their age or why they were aboard the *Devonia,* there was one thing that Stevenson and all there with him knew. Their futures were at best uncertain and would surely be hard. "Yet it must not be supposed that these people exhibited depression. The scene, on the contrary, was cheerful. Not a tear was shed on board the vessel. All were full of hope for the future, and showed an inclination to innocent gaiety. Some were heard to sing, and all began to scrape acquaintance with small jests and ready laughter."

A chessboard was brought out and before long two passengers were bent over it, engaged in fierce mental battle. In one part of the deck a lively card game was in progress, while not far away, fifteen people were playing a game of dominoes. Stevenson joined another, larger group.

"We got in a cluster like bees, sitting between each other's feet under the lee of the deck-houses. Stories and laughter went around. The children climbed about [the ship's railings and riggings]. . . . Lastly, down sat the fiddler in our midst and began to [play] his reels, and jigs, and ballads."

This merry and lively scene went on well into the afternoon, and Stevenson nearly forgot where he was—that is, until three first-class passengers appeared on deck. "A gentleman and two young ladies [picked] their way with little gracious titters of indulgence, which galled me to the quick. . . . It was astonishing what insults these people managed to convey by their presence. They seemed to throw their clothes in our faces. Their eyes searched us all over for tatters and incongruities. . . . We were in truth very innocently, cheerfully, and sensibly engaged, and there was no shadow of excuse for [their] swaying elegant superiority."

After making a quick tour of the steerage area, the three first-class passengers retreated to their clean cabins, well-prepared food, and servants. But the damage had been done. "We had been made to feel ourselves a sort of comical lower animal," Stevenson remembered angrily. "We were all conscious of an icy influence and a dead break in the course of our enjoyment."

Echoing the change in mood, the sky clouded over the next day. The wind picked up and rain, small and thick, began falling. Driven inside the airless hull of the ship once more, the steerage passengers did whatever they could to make themselves comfortable. For his part, Stevenson discovered that if he slept on the floor close to the door he could catch a thin draft of fresh air.

On the morning of the tenth day, the *Devonia* chugged into New York harbor. Not many of the steerage passengers rushed on deck to see the city's shoreline or to celebrate their arrival. The tossing ship and stale air had left most of them exhausted and ill. Besides, only about a third of them would be staying in New York. The rest still had hundreds or even thousands of miles of travel ahead of them.

In one respect, Stevenson was fortunate. Because he had paid an extra eight dollars for his tiny cabin, a city official came aboard to approve his entry into the United States. The other steerage passengers had to stay on the ship an additional night. In the morning, they would be herded to Castle Garden —the receiving station for emigrants before Ellis Island was

The long ocean voyage is over. Now these three weary women and a child must take their few belongings and go to be processed for entry.
(Museum of the City of New York)

built—where they would be interrogated and examined by a score of suspicious officials. There were no immigration quotas back then and few rules. To enter the United States, a person had to be physically and mentally healthy, and had to give officials an idea of where he or she planned to settle.

As Stevenson debarked from the ship, his pace was slow and deliberate, as if he were carrying a heavy weight. He was worried about Fanny, of course, and was anxious to get some word on her condition. In addition, the trip had left him weak and fourteen pounds lighter. He was also aware that the friendships formed during the harsh sea crossing were probably over, that his fellow travelers would soon disappear to the far corners of America to begin their new lives.

With obvious fondness Stevenson recalled the people he had met on the *Devonia*. "Some were handy, some intellectual, and almost all were pleasantly and kindly disposed. I had many long and serious talks, and many a good bout of mirth with my fellow passengers and I thought they formed, upon the whole, an agreeable and well informed society."

In this reflective mood, Stevenson made his way through the rainy night and flooded roadways of an unfamiliar city, searching for a cheap but clean hotel.

Looking dazed after their ocean voyage, three generations of a German family have stopped to ask directions to the train station. The sign on the wall promising a trip west "without change of cars" was somewhat misleading, since it was referring only to the New Jersey to Chicago part of the journey. (New-York Historical Society)

All Aboard!

S TEVENSON'S FIRST MORNING in the United States began with a window-rattling boom as a cannon was fired to announce the beginning of another day. After rubbing the sleep from his eyes, he discovered that rain was still coming down, only much heavier than the night before.

Since the train west was not scheduled to depart until the next morning, Stevenson had a free day to get chores done. After a large breakfast—the first really good meal he'd had since leaving Scotland—he set off for the post office. Before sailing, Stevenson had cabled the people caring for Fanny, telling them to send messages to the post offices of large cities along the route of his journey.

Stevenson's hotel was located on a narrow side street at the southern tip of New York, not far from Battery Park. It was a bustling commercial area then, filled with sturdy three- and four-story buildings that housed importers, booksellers, stables, print shops, and a variety of other small businesses and manufacturers. Large, horse-drawn wagons rumbled up and down the cobblestone streets, and people shouted to one another from doors and windows. Stevenson, head bent down against the rain, hardly noticed the activity around him.

"It rained with patient fury," he wrote, remembering the long walk to the post office. He hadn't thought to bring an umbrella on his journey and had so little cash that he couldn't afford the dollar fifty one would cost. Whenever the rain came down particularly hard, "I had to get under cover for a while . . . to give my mackintosh a rest; for under this continued drenching it began to grow damp on the inside."

At the post office he found a cable from California waiting for him in care of general delivery. He must hurry before it was too late, it said. "F. has inflammation of the brain."

Driven by his heightened concern, Stevenson rushed to a nearby bank to exchange his British pounds for American dollars, then went to the railroad offices to buy a ticket.

Railroad travel could be a complicated matter in the nineteenth century. There was no such thing as a nonstop trip from the East Coast to the West Coast in 1879, and each railroad company sold tickets for travel only on its own route. When one company's tracks ended, passengers had to gather up their baggage, walk to the next company's office, and buy a ticket for the next leg of their trip. Since many small companies owned only thirty or forty miles of track, a long trip could require eight or ten transfers. Stevenson was lucky, at least during the first leg of his journey. The Pennsylvania Railroad had recently bought and leased a number of other railroad lines, making it possible for a single ticket (which cost about twenty-four dollars) to cover a trip from New Jersey to Chicago.

After purchasing his ticket, Stevenson went to a nearby chemist's shop to see if he could get something to stop his itching. "My wrists were a mass of sores; so were many other parts of my body. The itching was at times overwhelming; at times, too, it was succeeded by furious stinging pains, like so many cuts from a carriage whip." Unfortunately the chemist misdiagnosed the cause of his problem and gave him powders to cure a liver ailment.

For the rest of the day, Stevenson investigated the city, wandering the narrow, twisting streets of lower Manhattan with rain as his only companion. Whenever he went into a shop, a pool of water would collect at his feet, "and those who were careful of their floors would look on with unfriendly eyes." Stevenson was excited to be in the United States and eager to learn as much as possible about the country and its people. His one extravagance that day was the purchase of six fat volumes of George Bancroft's *History of the United States,* which he planned to read on the train.

Back in his small room that night, an exhausted and very damp Stevenson fell asleep worrying about Fanny. It seemed as though he had barely put his head to the pillow when there was a pounding on his door. It was five o'clock in the morning, the hotel manager announced, and the ferry for New Jersey would be leaving in thirty minutes. He'd better hurry if he expected to get to Jersey City in time to catch his train.

Stevenson packed his belongings again, but he left behind all of the clothes he had worn the day before. They were so wet that "no fire could have dried them . . . and to pack them in their present condition was to spread ruin among my other possessions."

Despite the early hour, the darkness, and another day of persistent rain, the streets were swarming with people. Whole families lumbered along, bags, bundles, and babies in arm. Some had open carts filled to overflowing with furniture and trunks. In addition to the *Devonia,* three other emigrant ships had landed during the past two days, and it seemed as if all the passengers were headed for the one train scheduled to leave

A horse-drawn wagon piled high with the possessions of several families maneuvers through busy streets to the ferry dock. A sense of sadness clings to these travelers—they have left their past lives thousands of miles and an ocean behind them. (New-York Historical Society)

that day. Stevenson apparently did not encounter any of his fellow passengers from the *Devonia,* because he made no note of them in his journal.

Stevenson found himself swept along as if he were caught in a great rushing river that could not be stopped. At the pier, he purchased his ticket for the crossing (which cost about twenty cents) and followed the crowd onto the boat. "You may imagine how slowly this filtering proceeded, through the dense, choking crush, every one overladen with packages and children."

Stevenson had to stand on deck, but was able to escape the rain by huddling under a flimsy awning. The overcrowded ferry pulled away from the dock and steamed across the Hudson River to the railroad docks in New Jersey. "The landing at Jersey City was done in a stampede. . . . People pushed, and elbowed and ran, their families following how they could. Children fell, and were picked up, to be rewarded by a blow. I am ashamed to say that I ran among the rest."

His sprint from the pier to the train covered about one hundred yards, so by the time he got there he was soaked through once again. To make matters worse, the station had no waiting room and the doors to the cars were bolted. Stevenson, along with about three hundred other travelers, had to wait for over an hour on a long platform in the train shed. The platform was covered, so they were out of the direct rain, but a damp, cold wind whistled throughout the cavernous structure.

"I sat on my valise, too crushed to observe my neighbors," he remembered, "but as they were all cold, and wet, and weary, and driven stupidly crazy by the mismanagement to which we had been subjected, I believe they can have been no happier than myself."

This train on the New York and Harlem Line looks much like the one Stevenson boarded in Jersey City. The engine and coal tender are followed by a mail car, a freight car, and seven passenger cars. Even back in 1875, when this photo was taken, advertisements for an aperient (laxative) and hair color decorate a nearby fence. (New-York Historical Society)

While the passengers shivered on the platform, the train crew and station hands readied the train. The fireman shoveled coal into the furnace to keep steam pressure up; the engineer checked the gauges to make sure there was enough steam pressure and water. Clouds of white vapor escaped various gaskets and connections, hissing like an angry dragon.

Behind the engine, mail and manufactured goods were loaded aboard several freight cars; behind these cars baggage was being checked and tossed into the five baggage cars. Only after all of these cars were fully loaded were passengers finally allowed to board.

The car Stevenson found himself in was solidly built and very plain. A gas lamp burned feebly at either end of the car, and fifteen tiny windows ran its length, one to a seat. Most of the shivering passengers did not bother to open their windows, so the glass soon fogged over. Even though the seats were straight-backed and small, Stevenson made himself comfortable with some wiggling around.

He did not realize it at the time, but he would later view this

The first passenger car Stevenson boarded was probably a lot like this early Pullman car. When Pullman cars grew old and worn out, they were routinely reassigned to haul second-class and then, after being stripped of all decorative brass and woodwork, emigrant passengers. (Society of California Pioneers)

car as luxurious. Because the passengers with him included local businessmen and middle-class families, as well as the poor emigrants, the railroad had put on a slightly nicer type of passenger car than the emigrants usually got. The seats were lightly padded, the paint was fairly new, and the car had even been scrubbed out sometime during the past month.

Eventually, the conductor shouted "All aboard!" and the engineer opened the throttle. Steam pushed the driving cylinders into motion and the massive engine wheels began to move. With a jolt and a rattle, the cars trailing the engine started inching forward, their metal wheels grinding and squeaking on the iron tracks.

The train crept along at this slow pace for almost an hour. This was one of the busiest rail areas in the country, with a dizzying maze of tracks joining or crossing the main line. Signaling systems weren't always reliable at the time, so the engineer and fireman had to keep a sharp eye out for other trains on their track. In addition, the train occasionally traveled through city streets crowded with pedestrians, horse-drawn carriages, and stray animals. It wasn't until the train was well away from the urban areas that it picked up speed.

Stevenson busied himself by trying to brush his clothes dry, reading from Bancroft's *History of the United States,* and watching the passing scenery. The brick and stone structures of Jersey City eventually gave way to rolling woodlands of maples and pines, broken here and there by small farms and orchards. Every so often, the train came to a tiny hamlet and stopped to let off or take on commuting passengers, mail, and packages.

Most of these communities were too small to have a railroad station. The train simply stopped next to a flat clearing, and

During the early days of train travel, track frequently ran along busy main streets. (Author's collection)

passengers jumped from the high stairs to the ground. Many such places appeared along railroad tracks and were known as "borderland" towns—small pockets of family homes and businesses completely surrounded by forests or farms. As more and more people fled the crowded cities to live in such rural towns, these places grew in size, eating up the forests and farms. Nowadays, we refer to such communities as suburbs.

If Stevenson thought his trip west would move along

AHEAD OF THE WORLD !
THE GREAT AMERICAN FOUR TRACK RAILROAD.
LIGHTNING EXPRESS PASSENGER AND FREIGHT TRAINS; ALWAYS ON TIME.

The East Coast possessed some of the busiest and most congested railroad track in the world. Americans were extremely proud of their railroad system, as the title to this print makes clear. Needless to say, the guarantee of "Always On Time" applied to express trains only.
(Museum of the City of New York)

smoothly once in the countryside, he was sadly mistaken. They were between towns in New Jersey, surrounded by tangled woods, when the train stopped for no apparent reason and sat there for nearly a half hour. Just as suddenly, it started moving again. Several miles down the track, the train came to another halt. This time, it did not move again until darkness began to fall.

Each time the train stopped, the conductor popped his head into the car and announced that the passengers should prepare to leave the car and board a train on another track. He never told them why the train had stopped, and he never came back to tell them the order had been countermanded.

*   *   *

Stevenson had no way of knowing it, but a train wreck several hundred miles ahead had thrown the whole railroad line into chaos. Train wrecks were all too common in the nineteenth century—boilers blew up, decaying bridges collapsed under the weight of trains, brittle tracks cracked, wooden passenger cars were set on fire by kerosene lamps or wood heating stoves, brakes overheated and failed. Because of the primitive signal systems, two trains were often mistakenly switched onto the same track and sent speeding into each other. In 1875 alone, there were 104 head-on collisions in the United States.

As the disasters mounted, newspapers realized their readers wanted more information, so they began reporting on crashes in gory detail, usually providing a detailed illustration for added impact. The bigger crashes were given lurid names, such as the Camp Hill Disaster or the Angola Horror (where forty-two passengers were consumed by fire after their car fell off a bridge).

People were appalled and fascinated by train wrecks. Not long after a head-on collision took place in Pawtucket, Rhode Island, in 1856, an eager photographer made this picture of it. The print was rushed to an engraver, who made a black-and-white line drawing of the wreck. The line drawing appeared in newspapers around the country less than three days later. (George Eastman House)

No one realized that the old wooden truss bridge was in need of repair until this train fell through it in 1900. Miraculously, the train's last car teetered precariously on top of a stone foundation and its passengers escaped serious injury. (Smithsonian Institution)

The rushing water of a flash flood had undermined the foundation of this trestle—and sent the engineer and several passengers to a watery grave. (State Historical Society of Wisconsin)

Some accidents caught the imagination of the public and were turned into popular plays or songs. When engineer John Luther Jones failed to pay attention and rammed his locomotive into the rear of another train, his blunder was forgiven in a matter of days. In fact, he was honored for staying at the throttle of his engine in a tune called "Casey Jones."

Many people were outraged by the carnage on the rails and demanded better safety measures. A noted commentator of the time, George Templeton Strong, wrote, "Another railroad accident (so-called) on the Erie Road. Scores of people smashed, burned to death or maimed for life. We shall never travel safely till some pious, wealthy and much beloved railroad director has been hanged for murder."

Laws would be passed in the 1880s to force railroads to use better brakes and rails, and foolproof automatic signal devices. Train wrecks did decrease in number, but people's fascination with them never went away. In the 1890s, staged head-on collisions became a frequent form of entertainment. At one such event, thirty thousand spectators gathered to see two locomotives destroy each other in a steaming sixty-mile-per-hour crash. Even with such a humiliating end, the locomotives demonstrated their awesome power. The photographer of the event was blinded and a spectator standing almost three-quarters of a mile away was killed by flying bits of debris.

* * *

The wreck that was delaying Stevenson's train wasn't very big, but it still managed to back up traffic in all directions. Rerouting the many freight and passenger trains around the wreck was a complicated and painfully slow process. Stevenson's train wasn't considered important, so it had to pull onto side tracks frequently to let first-class express trains through.

*Illustrator Otto Stark has captured the dreadful moment when a
fast-moving express slammed into the rear of a freight train near
Steamburg, New York, in 1888.* (Author's collection)

The front cover to the October 1865 issue of Frank Leslie's Illustrated Newspaper *shows this train barreling through a forest fire. The engineer and fireman have already leapt to the safety of a riverbed, leaving the passengers to take care of themselves.*
(New-York Historical Society)

Much of Stevenson's trip would be wasted on side tracks as expresses sped past. In all, these little stops added up to nearly two days in lost time for him. He never tells readers what he felt about the fast-moving luxury trains, but he was probably angry and a bit envious, especially when they went by trailing the sound of music and laughter. The cramped and stifling box he was confined to was worlds apart from life on a Pullman Palace car.

*   *   *

George Mortimer Pullman began manufacturing experimental first-class passenger cars in 1864, five years before the transcontinental railroad was completed. Among his early innovations were the hinged upper sleeping berth that could be folded against the ceiling during the day, and the reclining seat, which could double as a bed (and meant that passengers didn't have to share bunks). Another of his improvements was the enclosed platform. This not only made walking from car to car safer, it protected travelers from rain, snow, and engine sparks.

By the time Stevenson was traveling, Pullman cars were large and airy, with oversize windows for easy viewing and deep, plush-cushioned seats. One contented rider wrote home, "I had a sofa to myself, with a table and a lamp. The sofas were widened and made into beds at night. My berth was three feet three inches wide, and six feet three inches long. It had two windows looking out of the train, a handsome mirror, and was well furnished with bedding and curtains."

The comfort and the fact that trains carrying first-class passengers were allowed to pass all other passenger and freight trains (cutting the cross-country journey down to a bearable six to seven days) made Pullman cars an instant hit. Their

A Pullman Palace car featured wide, cushioned chairs, large windows, and a big, airy space—nothing at all like Stevenson's car. (Denver Public Library)

Dining car service was first introduced in 1867, but did not become a regular feature until the late 1880s. Of course, dining cars were reserved for first-class passengers. Here a group of stockholders of a canal company await dinner. (Chicago Historical Society)

At first, many clergymen objected to having trains run on Sunday. Opposition vanished when railroads agreed to hold regular Sunday services, which included the singing of hymns accompanied by organ music. It did not hurt the railroad's position that it also established a policy of giving free passes to clergymen. (Library of Congress)

success was aided by the glowing praise of travel writers. After Frank Leslie and his staff took the journey in 1877, *Frank Leslie's Illustrated Newspaper* featured a story that concluded with, "A journey over the plains was [once] a formidable undertaking, that required great patience and endurance. Now all is changed. . . . The six months' journey is reduced to less than a week. The prairie schooner has passed away, and is replaced by the railway coach with all its modern comforts."

Of course, traveling on these cars cost extra. The price for the New York to Chicago portion of the trip might be as much as one hundred dollars, or four times as much as Stevenson paid. If a passenger wanted a private car for his or her family and friends, the fee was just over one hundred dollars *per day*. Most highly skilled Americans earned well under twelve hundred dollars a year, and yet people lined up to experience this unique form of luxury travel.

With first-class business booming, the railroads pressed Pullman to create even grander cars—and he responded with cars specifically designed for smoking, reading, listening to music, or just sitting back to relax. Each was hand-crafted to exacting standards and had, as one passenger recalled, "oiled walnut, carved and gilded, etched and stained plate glass, metal trappings heavily silver-plated, seats cushioned with thick plushes, washstands of marble and walnut, damask curtains, and massive mirrors in frames of gilded walnut. The floors are carpeted . . . and the roof beautifully frescoed in mosaics of gold, emerald-green, crimson, sky-blue, violet, drab and black."

While Stevenson and his fellow travelers may have grumped about the ostentatious opulence of first-class cars and the way their passengers were pampered, most Americans did not. Pullman Palace cars were a genuine source of pride for most citizens—a symbol of America's manufacturing supremacy, something their country and no other country in the world could produce. Noted writer and editor William Dean Howells summed it up when he said: "[Americans] surveyed with infinite satisfaction the elegance of the flying parlor in which they sat. . . . They said that none but Americans or enchanted princes in the Arabian Nights ever travelled in such state."

*   *   *

Near midnight, Stevenson's train crept through the city of Philadelphia and began to chug across the Pennsylvania countryside. Most of his fellow passengers had gone to sleep hours before, so Stevenson also leaned back and closed his eyes.

When he awoke the next day, the train was only about twenty miles outside of Philadelphia, though it was moving swiftly, passing one station after another without stopping. The train had spent the night creeping along slowly due to the accident, and now the engineer wanted to make up for as much of the lost time as possible. "We paid for this in the flesh," Stevenson noted, "for we had no meals all that day."

Still, the morning had brought with it something almost as precious—dry, sunny weather. "Our American sunrise had ushered in a noble summer's day. There was not a cloud; the sunshine was baking; yet in the woody river-valleys among which we wound our way the atmosphere preserved a sparkling freshness. . . . It had an inland sweetness and variety to one newly from the sea; it smelt of woods, rivers, and the delved earth."

Tired of sitting, Stevenson made his way to the small platform at the back of the last car to watch the countryside slide by. "A green, open, undulating country stretched away upon all sides," he recalled. "I saw, one after another, pleasant villages, carts upon the highway and fishers by the stream."

Mobile hunting lodges could be rented, and came complete with gun cases, dog kennels, and refrigerators for dead game. Jerome Marble (in the foreground to the right) rented this lodge for a hunting vacation on the Dakota prairie in 1876. (Minnesota Historical Society)

Having left the congested urban areas behind, two express trains race through the night. This well-known Currier & Ives print was done by the most famous illustrator of trains in the nineteenth century, Fanny Palmer. (Museum of the City of New York)

Stevenson's concern for Fanny accompanied him every mile of the way, but the fact that he was, at last, heading west at a steady rate let him relax a little and enjoy the experience of traveling. When the train crossed a metal bridge spanning a wide river, Stevenson leaned over the platform railing to ask the brakeman sitting on the roof the river's name. The brakeman shouted back, "The Susquehanna River."

"The beauty of the name seemed to be a part of the beauty of the land," Stevenson said, adding, "There is no part of the world where [the names are] so rich, poetical, humorous, and picturesque as the United States of America. All times, races, and languages have brought their contributions. . . . The names of the States and Territories themselves form a chorus of sweet and most romantic vocables: Delaware, Ohio, Indiana, Florida, Dakota, Iowa, Wyoming, Minnesota, and the Carolinas; there are few poems with nobler music to the ear; a songful, tuneful land."

It was while he was in this blissful mood that his train pulled into the city of Pittsburgh, and a very hungry Stevenson stumbled off the car and went in search of the post office and a meal.

An engineer was assigned only one engine, and many looked on their engines as their own personal property. This drawing shows an engine cab modestly decked out with sprigs of holly for Christmas. Some engineers decorated much more elaborately. One engineer, "Bat" Casey, outfitted his cab with a Seth Thomas clock, mahogany seat boxes with red cushions, a linoleum floor, and a stag's head. He even had several levers and pipes nickel-plated. (Author's collection)

Aboard the
Emigrant Train

AFTER PITTSBURGH, Stevenson's train hurried west at a steadier pace, the clickey-clack of wheels hitting rail joinings adding a jittery background noise to the ride. When they left Pennsylvania and entered Ohio, the terrain began to level out.

On these long, straight stretches of track, the train was often able to top sixty miles per hour. This was the astonishing speed that so impressed anyone who saw or rode the rails. One such person was frontiersman Davy Crockett. Commenting on this memorable aspect of his first train ride in 1820, he said, "I can only judge the speed by putting my head out [the window] to spit, which I did, and overtook it so quick that it hit me smack in the face." Soon railroad companies began placing spittoons in all cars and advising passengers to spit in them and not out the window.

Stevenson used the windows strictly to view the passing countryside and was delighted at what he saw. "Ohio was not at all what I had pictured. We were now on those great plains which stretch unbroken to the Rocky Mountains. The country was flat like Holland, but far from being dull. All through Ohio, Indiana, Illinois, and Iowa . . . it was rich and various, and breathed an elegance peculiar to itself. The tall corn pleased the eye; the trees were graceful in themselves, and framed the plain into long, aerial vistas; and the clean, bright, gardened townships spoke of country fare and pleasant summer evenings."

There were only two bothersome aspects to this part of the trip. Each morning, a freezing chill invaded the car and caused Stevenson to shiver uncontrollably. Then there were the frequent advertisements set up facing the tracks. "The fences along the line bore but two descriptions of advertisement; one to recommend tobaccos, and the other to vaunt remedies against the ague."

It was somewhere in Ohio or Indiana that Stevenson developed a severe case of diarrhea. During one of the brief meal stops, it's likely that he was served spoiled food, all too common an experience for transcontinental travelers. More than half the passengers on Stevenson's train came down with food poisoning at one time or another during the journey.

The sun had set by the time they arrived at Chicago, the end of the first part of the long cross-country trip. "I was hot, feverish, painfully athirst; and there was a great darkness over me, an internal darkness, not to be dispelled."

The post office was closed, so there was no possibility of getting word about Fanny's health. In the gloom of darkness, an exhausted and ill Stevenson gathered up his belongings—including his six ponderous volumes of Bancroft—and made his way to the next train station, which was about a mile away.

Less than nine years had passed since a wind-driven fire had destroyed over seventeen thousand buildings in Chicago and left ninety-eight thousand people homeless. Newspapers in many countries had reported on the terrible fire, and people from around the world—including Stevenson—had sent con-

*Chicago Station bustles with passengers and activity. The frontiers-
man and Native Americans (right) were added to the picture to show
how close Chicago was to the wilderness.* (Chicago Historical Society)

tributions to aid in the city's rebuilding. Chicago had responded to the challenge of rebuilding with amazing energy,
literally sweeping the burned-out area clean of every trace of
the fire and erecting bigger and grander structures. Now, as
he went down streets of sturdy brick office buildings and pros-
perous stone houses, Stevenson thought, "It would be a graceful act for the [city] to refund that sixpence, or, at the least, to
entertain me to a cheerful dinner. But there was no word of
restitution . . . and the best dinner I could get was a dish of
ham and eggs at my own expense."

At the next station, he bought a ticket for the second leg of
his journey (for about twenty dollars), then sat in a dark,
crowded waiting room while his train was being put together.
"When it was time to start, I descended the platform like a
man in a dream. It was a long train, lighted from end to end;
and car after car, as I came upon it, was not only filled, but
overflowing. . . . When at last I found an empty bench, I sank
into it like a bundle of rags; the world seemed to swim away

into the distance, and my consciousness dwindled within me to a mere pin's head."

While Stevenson was settling in, another passenger plopped down next to him. "I found that there had sat beside me a very cheerful, rosy little German gentleman, somewhat gone to drink, who was talking away to me."

The train was soon on its way, and Stevenson discovered he was the target of a one-sided conversation with his traveling companion. The man spoke so rapidly, and changed subjects so often, that Stevenson was overwhelmed and confused. "I did my best to keep up the conversation; for it seemed to me dimly as if something depended upon that . . . but though I caught the words, I do not think I properly understood the sense. I remember a gabbling sound of words, his profuse gesticulation, and his smile; but no more."

A few towns down the track, the German gentleman left the train, and Stevenson was able to lean back in silence and sleep the rest of the night away. Even as Stevenson slept, the train made stop after stop. His was a journey that consisted of hundreds of stops. Many were made so that commuters between stations could get off. The majority of stops were made for emigrants.

* * *

Of the sixteen and a half million emigrants who came to the United States during the second half of the nineteenth century, approximately one-third would settle in the cities where their ships docked, such as New York, Boston, or Charleston. That means that almost eleven million emigrants boarded trains to find their new homes.

Add to them legions of American citizens who wanted to relocate in the West, too. At one point, Stevenson took time to study who was riding in the car with him. In addition to foreigners, he noted that "all the States of the North had sent out a fugitive to cross the plains with me—from Virginia, from Pennsylvania, from New York, from far western Iowa and Kansas, from Maine that borders on the Canadas, and from the Canadas themselves."

Very few families or individuals set up home in a place where they did not know someone. Most settled in areas where they had relatives and friends or where people knew their language and customs or practiced the same religion. Communities of German, Irish, Swedish, Russian, English, French, Italian, Scottish, and Polish emigrants, not to mention a variety of religious sects, blossomed in state after state. Most blacks,

An immigrant family waiting for relatives to pick them up on the platform in Minneapolis. (Minnesota Historical Society)

A group of Russian Germans arriving in Lincoln, Nebraska. (Nebraska State Historical Society)

fleeing the war-torn south, set up homes in large western cities, such as Chicago, but a significant number made their way into rural areas of Wisconsin, Nebraska, and the Dakotas. These ethnic and religious pockets gave people an instant sense of community and well-being, not to mention some friendly advice on what to expect in the days and months ahead.

Russian Mennonites who had been talked into coming to America by railroad agent C. B. Schmidt proved to be extremely good at helping one another. Between 1873 and 1883, approximately eighteen thousand fled Russia for America, with over ten thousand ending up in Kansas. Those following the first wave of settlers got off the train to discover a large dormitory waiting for them. There they could rest and refresh themselves, and spend a few days curing whatever illnesses they might have contracted since leaving their homeland. They could also pick up valuable information about where the choicest areas to settle were, what to expect in terms of weather, and which crops to grow.

Needless to say, a warm welcome did not guarantee success for any of the arriving emigrants. Almost 25 percent of all emigrants would fail at their new lives and be forced to leave (a few to return to their native countries, most to head to the closest large city where jobs were more plentiful). But the majority stayed—through viciously cold winters, summer droughts, hungry waves of grasshoppers, and personal tragedies—and many of the communities established over one hundred years ago still prosper today.

"We gave [the railroads] an empire composed of an arid desert unfit for the habitation of man," wrote Congressman Charles E. Hooker. And in return, they gave the nation "an empire of hardy and industrious citizens."

*   *   *

Sometimes the men in a family came to America alone to purchase land, build a house, and plant crops. Later, after selling some of their harvest, they sent for the rest of the family. Here, the Perry brothers spend a Sunday afternoon relaxing with watermelon and cards. (Nebraska State Historical Society)

Three generations of the Shores family pose in front of their sod homes near Westerville, Nebraska. They would eventually become famous as musicians. (Nebraska State Historical Society)

Russian Mennonites were greeted at the station and taken to a dormitory to rest before setting out for their new homes. Not only were they able to meet people who spoke their language and could give them helpful hints about America, they could also wash off some of the grime from their long journey. (New-York Historical Society)

Martha and Notley Henderson, along with their three children. The Hendersons fled the South shortly after the Civil War and settled in Madison Township, Wisconsin, where they prospered. (State Historical Society of Wisconsin)

Ernest Valeton de Boissière (with white beard) established a communal French colony in 1869 in Franklin County, Kansas. These settlers produced high-quality silk until cheaper foreign competition forced them to switch to dairy products. (Kansas State Historical Society)

Large numbers of Swedish emigrants came to America in the 1870s and 1880s. This group, out for a Sunday picnic, is from Greeley County, Kansas. (Kansas State Historical Society)

A wedding party of Germans from Cheney, Kansas, take time out from the celebration to have a group portrait made. The 'happy' bride and groom stand in the center, wearing sashes. (Kansas State Historical Society)

Alsatians in native costumes just outside the Union Depot in St. Paul, Minnesota. (Minnesota Historical Society)

Unlike settlers on the prairie grasslands, the Wickstrom family found plenty of timber for their solid log cabin in Fence, Wisconsin. (State Historical Society of Wisconsin)

A day and a half later, Stevenson's train arrived at the Pacific Transfer Station near Council Bluffs, Iowa, where "I gave way to a thirst for luxury . . . and marched with my effects into the Union Pacific Hotel" for a good night's sleep. This rest did settle his stomach to a degree, but the effects of the food poisoning would haunt him throughout the rest of his trip.

The following afternoon, Stevenson went to the train station and waited with "more than a hundred others, to be sorted and boxed for the [rest of the] journey."

Hotels in the West were never very elegant, as this 1901 photograph of the lobby of the Teller House in Central City, Colorado, makes clear. The writing desk (right) contains advertisements for local stores, while spittoons (left) line the clerk's desk. (Colorado Historical Society)

The clerks at this Union Pacific station in Kansas City, Missouri, look downright suspicious as they stare into the camera. (Union Pacific Museum Collection)

So far, his trip had been on trains where middle-class passengers and poorer emigrants traveled together. These were commonly referred to as mixed trains. The train out of Council Bluffs would have only emigrants in it. As if to reinforce the low status of its passengers, the words EMIGRANT CAR were painted in large yellow letters across the side of the train.

Emigrants paid very little for their tickets (it cost around forty dollars to go from Iowa to Sacramento), and the railroad company made no effort at all to make them feel welcomed or comfortable. Even boarding the train was a chore.

"A white-haired official, with a stick under one arm, and a list in the other hand, stood apart from us, and called name after name in the tone of a command. At each name you would see a family gather up its brats and bundles and run for the

The platform is once again crowded with colorful characters as passengers prepare to board a Union Pacific train. The two N's in the Union Pacific sign were printed backward to draw attention to the name. (Nebraska State Historical Society)

hindmost of the three cars that stood awaiting us, and I soon concluded it was . . . set apart for the women and children. The second car . . . was devoted to men travelling alone, and the third to the Chinese. The official was easily moved to anger at the least delay; but the emigrants were both quick at answering their names, and speedy in getting themselves and their effects on board."

The passenger cars Stevenson had been on before this were at best cramped and dim and stifling. The car he entered at Council Bluffs was far worse. It was "only remarkable for [its] extreme plainness . . . [a] long, narrow wooden box, like a flat-roofed Noah's ark."

At one end of the car a wood-burning stove stood on a tiny platform. An enclosed space at the other end held the toilet, which was referred to as the "convenience" or the "retiring room." Several oil wall lamps gave off feeble illumination. But what drew Stevenson's attention was the seats.

Five days of sitting on thinly padded cushions, his knees rubbing and bumping into the seats in front, had left him bruised and sore. The new seating arrangements were a horror. "The benches are too short for anything but a young child. Where there is scarce elbow-room for two to sit, there will not be space for one to lie."

Having loaded on the human cargo, the train crew began to make up the rest of the train. No one was allowed to leave the train, so all the passengers sat in their narrow seats as one baggage car after another was filled and coupled to the train. Four hours later, the twentieth—and last—baggage car was attached and "the long train crawled out of the Transfer Station and across the wide Missouri River to Omaha, westward bound."

*   *   *

When Stevenson traveled, the United States boasted more railroad track than any other country in the world—over ninety-three thousand miles of it. Almost all of this track was east of the Mississippi River, a vast spiderweb of iron that linked the smallest rural villages to the biggest cities. West of the Mississippi, less and less track existed until only a single line of track seventeen hundred miles long ran from Nebraska to California.

Work on this first transcontinental railroad began officially in 1863, though no real progress was made until the end of the Civil War two years later. The job was so enormous that two companies had to be created to handle it. The Union Pacific started from Omaha, Nebraska, and laid track westward, while the Central Pacific began construction in Sacramento, California, and headed east. The plan was for them to meet somewhere in Nevada.

History books generally focus on the men who owned and operated these companies, justly praising their foresight and daring, and, ultimately, damning their greed for stealing millions of dollars from the government. But the real heroes of the transcontinental railroad were the workers who blasted out the tunnels, graded the hard earth, and nailed the iron into place. Almost all of it by hand.

Who were these people? The Union Pacific work force was made up of Union and Confederate soldiers fresh from the Civil War, blacks fleeing the South, failed farmers and prospectors, a scattering of Native Americans, and even a few women. The largest number of Union Pacific workers were immigrants from Ireland. The Central Pacific relied almost exclusively on the muscle of Chinese laborers.

The working patterns for the Union and Central Pacific were very similar. Surveyors led the way, combing rugged moun-

Construction Superintendent for the Union Pacific, Samuel Reed, gazes down a line of ties that stretches to the horizon. (Library of Congress)

This rare picture shows a crew of black construction workers positioning a rail before spiking it in place. (Oakland Museum)

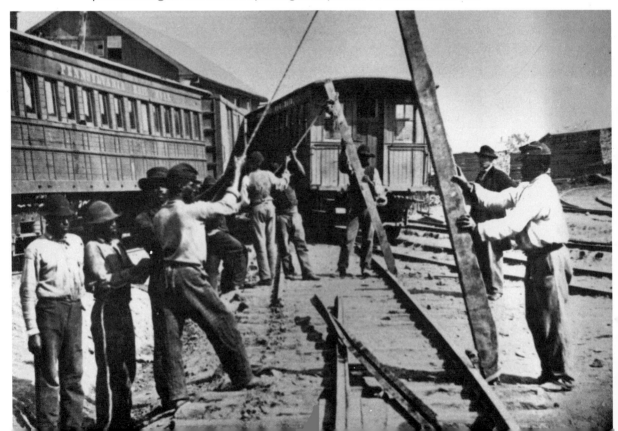

tains and tangled forests for the easiest routes. Following the surveyors were location men who staked out the exact grades and curves the track would take. Next came the graders; using horse and mule power, picks and shovels and a lot of sweat, they sculpted a path for the tracks. Behind them, the bridge monkeys erected trestles across rivers and gullies. And, of course, a small army of men was needed to feed, clothe, and guard the work crews. It was the tracklayers, however, who captured the imagination of observers.

Wooden ties were hauled in by wagon and dropped into place, five for every twenty-eight feet of rail, and stretching out for as far as the eye could see. A horse-drawn flatcar brought in the iron rails, stopping where the last track had been laid in place. Then the men took over.

Each rail weighed from five hundred to seven hundred pounds and required five men to lift and put in place. The clampers and spikers went to work immediately—thirty spikes to a rail, three blows to drive the spike in solid. Each rail took precisely thirty seconds to position and spike, and if a man was injured during the process, another took his place instantly and the work went on. Even as the clampers and spikers were fastening the rail down, the flatcar would be rolling forward on it, and the procedure was repeated.

And so the work went on, day after day, through searing heat, driving rainstorms, and blizzards. Early on in the construction, crews were able to lay about a mile of track per day. Later, they were averaging between two and three miles. On one incredible day, April 28, 1869, the Chinese tracklayers were able to spike ten miles of track in the space of ten hours. They had positioned over twenty-five thousand ties and thirty-five hundred rails, fastening them with twenty-eight thousand spikes and fourteen thousand bolts. No wonder that a newspaper writer witnessing work on the railroad said, "A grand

The paymaster's car has arrived and the men have gathered to collect their wages. Sitting on top of the car (far left), his hat tilted at a jaunty angle, is one of the few boys who managed to secure work as a tracklayer. (Union Pacific Museum Collection)

Anvil Chorus [is] playing across the plains. . . . 1800 miles to San Francisco—21,000,000 times those sledges [will be] swung; 21,000,000 times are they to come down with their punctuation before the great work of modern America is complete."

The Union Pacific and Central Pacific tracks finally met and were joined along a desolate stretch of Utah (not in Nevada, as originally intended) in 1869. This first transcontinental railroad was an immediate success and other railroad companies began building routes to connect the remaining sections of the

West. The Southern Pacific (1883), the Northern Pacific (1883), the Atchison, Topeka and Santa Fe (1885), and the Great Northern (1893), as well as hundreds of branch routes, added over seventy thousand miles of track to the United States total, bringing it to one hundred sixty-six thousand miles.

People in the United States took great pride in their railroad system. "I felt patriotically proud," a traveler to California said. The transcontinental railroad had bound the Union together "by links of iron that can never be broken."

As for the owners of these railroads, most profited hand-

The track heads across the vast prairie while workers scurry about like so many ants. To the right of the track, wagons are a blur as they hasten forward with loads of wooden ties. Despite the clatter and commotion, one worker manages to take a nap on the flatcar nearest the camera. (Minnesota Historical Society)

Railroad workers pause for the camera, along with some Native American families who happened to be traveling near the construction site. Workers were housed in two-story-tall dormitory cars, where sanitary conditions were awful. E. C. Lockwood remembered sleeping on top of the cars because "to tell the truth, we were troubled by cooties." (Minnesota Historical Society)

somely, becoming millionaires many times over. Even the foremen of the work crews did very well. One, John Stephen Casement, received seven hundred fifty dollars for every mile of track his crews were able to complete. And the workers? For their sweat and blood, they earned an average of about a dollar fifty per day, plus bed and board.

* * *

Stevenson had followed the building of the transcontinental railroad in European newspapers, and he might have read about it in Bancroft's book, but he makes no mention of the achievement in his journal. A lot of his attention was focused on making himself as comfortable as possible, or watching a dark line of clouds in the distance.

Night came on and the lamps were lit. "It was a troubled, uncomfortable evening in the cars. There was thunder in the air, which helped to keep us restless. A party of wild young men . . . stood together on the stern platform [outside the car], singing 'The Sweet By-and-By' with tuneful voices." When they got off at their stop, a man with a cornet began playing tunes. No one paid much attention to him until he came to "Home Sweet Home."

The song apparently reminded many of the travelers of their homelands. Stevenson noticed that several of them began to cry. They probably would have wallowed in these feelings if it hadn't been for "an elderly, hard-looking man, with a goatee beard, [who] turned with a start and bade the performer to stop that 'damned thing. I've heard enough of that.' The performer took the instrument from his lips, laughed and nodded, and then struck into a dance measure."

The train raced across Nebraska, stopping every so often to let passengers off, and, gradually, as another day came to an

It's nighttime, and emigrant-car passengers twist and turn to find a comfortable sleeping position. The conductor is trying to wake one sleeper to make room for a new arrival. (Denver Public Library)

end, travelers began getting ready for sleep. This was when Stevenson learned a valuable technique to make his nights a bit more comfortable—something called chumming.

When he had boarded the train, the conductor had sold him a piece of board and three straw cushions for two dollars and fifty cents. "The benches can be made to face each other in pairs, for the backs are reversible. On the approach of night the boards are laid from bench to bench, making a couch wide enough for two, and long enough for a man of the middle height."

Finding an instant chum was the next step. Stevenson recalled that the conductor "made a most active master of ceremonies, introducing likely couples, and even guaranteeing the amiability and honesty of each."

Emigrant cars were crowded and uncomfortable, but at least each passenger got a seat. This train is packed to overflowing with eager homesteaders heading to the Cherokee Strip in Oklahoma in 1889. Because the railroad company had already filled up all of its passenger cars, it had to use cattle cars instead. (Chicago, Rock Island & Pacific Railroad)

The big cities and crowds have been left behind as a passenger train steams through a tiny village and heads across an empty landscape. This picture was also done by the extremely talented Fanny Palmer and was the most popular Currier & Ives train print ever produced. (Museum of the City of New York)

Unfortunately, his first prospective chum, an elderly, heavy-set man from New England, rejected Stevenson the moment he saw him. With Stevenson standing there, the man told the conductor that "he didn't know the young man. . . . The young man might be very honest, but how was he to know that? There was another young man whom he had met already in the train; he guessed *he* was honest, and would prefer to chum with *him* upon the whole."

Stevenson began to worry that no one would be willing to chum with him, when "a tall, strapping, long-limbed, small-headed, curly-haired Pennsylvania Dutchman" stepped forward and volunteered. They made an odd couple: the shorter Stevenson curled himself into an uncomfortably tight ball so he fit within the space allotted, while the Dutchman sprawled, all feet and knees, his head leaning over the back of the bench.

As midnight approached, bolts of lightning flashed across the evening sky. The gloomy weather that had clung to Stevenson at the start of his journey had caught up with him again. Surrounded by the sounds of rain striking the top of the car, the snoring of his fellow travelers, and dark, troubling thoughts about Fanny's health, Stevenson drifted off to an uneasy sleep. He had completed five days of cross-country train travel; seven more lay ahead of him.

Newsboys would sell anything a passenger needed—books, newspapers, sandwiches, even ice water. An energetic newsboy could make up to eighty dollars in a week, which was a great deal of money when you consider that the engineer made only about sixty dollars a month. (Author's collection)

4

Into the Wild West

STEVENSON WOKE UP the next morning before sunrise, just as the train was pulling into a station. Shortly after it stopped, the door to the car opened and a boy of twelve burst in carrying a large box.

"A great personage on an American train is the newsboy. He sells books (such books!), papers, fruits, lollipops, and cigars . . . soap, towels, tin washing-dishes, tin coffee pitchers, coffee, tea, sugar, and tinned eatables, mostly hash or beans and bacon."

Almost immediately, Stevenson discovered that chumming (this time, three-way chumming) was the most economical way to wash and eat. He and his Pennsylvania bed-chum found a friendly young man from Dubuque, Iowa, and became "the firm of Pennsylvania, Shakespeare, and Dubuque. Shakespeare was my own nickname on the cars."

Their first order of business was to purchase supplies from the newsboy. "Shakespeare bought a tin washing-dish; Dubuque a towel, and Pennsylvania a brick of soap. The partners used these instruments, one after the other, according to the order of their first awaking."

Because they got up before anyone else, washing inside the car was just about impossible. All benches were taken and the floor was crowded with sleeping travelers and bundles. Even the convenience wouldn't do. It had no window and no gaslight. Stevenson and his chums, however, were clever enough to find a solution.

"Each filled the tin dish at the water filter opposite the stove, and retired with the whole stock in trade to the [rear] platform of the car. There he knelt down, supporting himself by a shoulder against the woodwork, or one elbow crooked about the railing, and made a shift to wash his face and neck and hands —a cold, an insufficient, and, if the train is moving rapidly, a somewhat dangerous toilet."

The same sort of teamwork went into getting breakfast ready. The cost of buying the eggs, coffee, coffee cake, and pans was shared equally, as were the cooking chores at the heating stove. When everything was prepared, Shakespeare, Pennsylvania, and Dubuque, using the bedboard as a table, sat sipping their coffee and chatting as the sun slowly rose. "It was," Stevenson would recall, "the pleasantest hour of the day."

After the calm of breakfast, the real travel day began. Other passengers began to wake up and move around the car; children from the next car ran up and down the aisle, screaming and crying; breakfasts were cooked, filling the interior with the smell of garlic, onions, and sausages. Cigar and cigarette smoke drove out the last traces of fresh air. And, as always, there was the numbing rumble of the train as it toiled along, mile after mile, "like a snail."

Fortunately for Stevenson, few safety rules were in effect when he rode the train across the continent. As long as he was willing to risk the dangers, he could go anywhere he wanted on—*or above*—the train. To escape the stifling atmosphere inside the passenger car, Stevenson climbed the ladder on the rear platform to the car's roof and made his way forward to the roof of a freight car loaded with fruit. There he sat for hours on end, thinking about Fanny and watching the Nebraska landscape pass by.

"The green plain ran till it touched the skirts of heaven. Along the track innumerable wild sunflowers, no bigger than a crown-piece, bloomed in a continuous flower-bed; now and again we might perceive a few dots beside the railroad, which grew more and more distinct as we drew nearer, till they turned into wooden cabins, and then dwindled and dwindled in our wake until they melted into their surroundings, and we were once more alone upon the billiard-table."

* * *

While he mentions seeing a few "grazing animals," Stevenson makes no mention of one of America's most famous animals, the bison (sometimes referred to by their Old World name of buffalo). Over twelve million bison roamed the West when work on the first transcontinental railroad began in 1863. Sometimes a single herd would be so large that the vast landscape of the plains was filled with them for as far as the eye could see. By the time Stevenson's train chugged through sixteen years later, only about one hundred fifty thousand bison remained.

What happened to these great herds? The first deadly assault on them came in the 1830s and 1840s and was carried out by Native Americans. In addition to hunting enough bison for their own needs, members of several tribes discovered that they could trade hides for rifles, ammunition, kitchenware, clothing, and other items. Records for the American Fur Com-

The train has stopped and frenzied passengers hurry from it to shoot at a herd of bison. Even the engineer (in the center, leaning from the engine cab) has his rifle aimed at a fleeing animal. (Library of Congress)

pany show that over one hundred thousand hides a year were bought from Native American hunters. Another company reported similar quantities being turned in at Bent's Fort, Colorado.

While these totals are significant, they were nothing compared to the slaughter carried out later for the railroad companies. Over ten thousand men were employed by the Union and Central Pacific Railroads and, to feed this army, contractors were hired to provide tons of bison meat per day. Sharpshooters stalked the herds on horseback, shooting any bison they could get their sights on, even pregnant cows. The most famous of these hunters was a former Pony Express rider named William F. Cody, whose hunting skills earned him the nickname Buffalo Bill.

As with many Western legends, the truth about Cody's shooting skill was greatly exaggerated. Hunting bison, especially during the early years when herds were very large, was relatively easy. The weapons of choice back then were the Sharps .45-caliber and the Remington .50-caliber rifles, both of which could kill at a distance of forty-five hundred feet. All a hunter had to do was point his rifle in the general direction of a herd and fire as many times as possible before the animals finally got scared and fled. An army captain, Randolph B. Marcy, spoke about this in his book *The Prairie Traveler:* "A Delaware Indian and myself once killed five buffalo out of a small herd before the remainder were so much as disturbed as to move away; the reports of our rifles did not disturb them in the least, and they continued grazing during all the time we were loading and firing."

Even as the slaughter for the railroad went on, another wave of killings was taking place, this one at the hands of cattle ranchers. Cattle ranching was already a booming business in the West when the railroads came through. Trains made shipping to eastern markets simpler and cheaper, and ranches grew larger. To ranchers, bison were big, useless animals that were eating their grass, so they hired sharpshooters to clear the land.

If this weren't enough, even travelers to the West felt a need to kill bison. Obliging engineers often stopped their trains when they came to a herd to enable tourists to take a few potshots at the animals. If the train didn't stop, eager travelers

A mound of approximately forty thousand bison hides waiting to be processed in Dodge City, Kansas, in 1874. (Kansas State Historical Society)

would fire through open windows and from car platforms. Hardly any of the tourists bothered to pick up what they killed or to use the carcass in any way.

The final threat to the animal came from various businesses. Stuffed bison heads were prized souvenirs for tourists, and many people wanted a bison skin for their winter sleigh rides or a bison rug for their parlors. Pickled bison tongue was considered a great delicacy on the East Coast. Skulls and bones

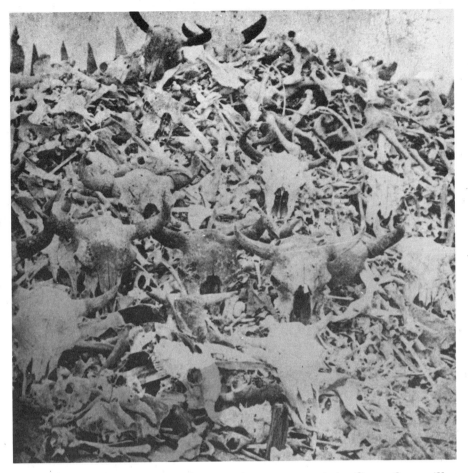

These skulls and bones make a grotesque mountain. Soon they will be ground into a fine powder for use in the manufacture of bone china or as fertilizer. (Kansas State Historical Society)

were ground up for fertilizer or used in the manufacture of bone china. A lot of meat went to feed railroad workers and, later, the passing travelers, but most of it was left on the plains to rot.

Bison weren't the only targets for sharpshooters and amateur hunters. Anything that roamed or flew too close to the tracks was a potential target—antelope, blacktail deer, wolves, rabbits, foxes, ducks, geese, and passenger pigeons.

When the hunting lust ran particularly high, some greenhorn travelers would even shoot at cattle and, incidentally, at the men tending them.

Bison and other game began to disappear rapidly from the West. Few ranchers and settlers were upset by this; after all, the grasslands were now filled with herds of beef cattle, so their food supply was safe. But Native Americans, who depended on bison for food, clothing, and many other items, felt their disappearance severely. "Wherever the whites are established," the Sioux chief White Cloud said bitterly, "the red hunters must die of hunger."

Fresh bison hides have been stretched out for drying, while (on the right) three men use all of their strength to compress a pile of dried hides so they can be tied into convenient bundles. A pile of skulls and bones (background) awaits the grinding process. (Kansas State Historical Society)

Bison weren't the only animals hunted in the West. Here, hunters near Webster, South Dakota, pose with the animals they shot in a single day in 1888. (New-York Historical Society)

Native Americans attempted to resist the invasion of their lands and the killing of the bison, but with little success. Eventually, with their source of food almost entirely destroyed, the great hunting tribes were forced onto government reservations.

As for the bison, the hunting continued until fewer than one thousand existed in 1900. They were such a rarity that when a lone bison wandered near a small town in Wyoming early in the twentieth century, the entire population went out to view it. The people stared at the creature for a long while and then, because no one knew what else to do, someone shot it. In time, a crusade to rescue the bison from extinction was begun, and now more than thirty thousand roam through various national parks and private rangelands. Gone, however, are the giant herds that stretched for fifty miles and, when the animals stampeded, could cause the earth to shake and rumble.

*   *   *

Without the herds of bison, the scene Stevenson saw from the top of the train was flat and bleak. "It was a world almost without a feature; an empty sky, an empty earth; front and back, the line of railway stretched from horizon to horizon, like a cue across a billiard-board."

The only break in the monotony came from the numerous halts the train made. In addition to pulling over for express trains, they had to take on water and fuel every forty or fifty miles. There were also more than two hundred railroad stations between the Transfer Station and California. Of course, they also had to stop in towns to let travelers get something to eat. Since the emigrant train did not travel at the convenience of its passengers, meal stops were never made on a regular schedule. After breakfast came "a dinner somewhere between

Whenever a train came into a western town, a crowd gathered to greet friends and relatives, pick up packages, or just plain hang around. This photograph of the station at Topeka, Kansas, was taken in 1880 from the top of a freight car. (Kansas State Historical Society)

This Harper's Weekly *illustration from 1876 shows the chaos and all-around bad manners of a meal stop on the transcontinental railroad.* (New-York Historical Society)

eleven and two, and supper from five to eight or nine at night. We had . . . less than twenty minutes for each."

Time during stops was extremely precious, so passengers would exit the train in a rush and hurry to the closest restaurant. After the first day, travelers learned that the secret of successful dining was to enter the eating establishment on the run and immediately yell out their order, grabbing an empty table at the same time.

A chaotic scene usually followed as more and more travelers jammed into the room, waiters pushed their way through the crowd with overloaded trays, diners shoveled in food or tried to get their waiter to get them another cup of coffee. The only consolation for this inconvenience was that passengers on emigrant trains paid less for their meals than other travelers. A meal that normally went for two dollars cost emigrants only one dollar, and some establishments reduced the price to seventy-five cents if payment was made in silver instead of paper money.

Stevenson had little to say about his transcontinental meals, probably because his stomach virus had worsened and made eating unpleasant. "The meals, taken overland, were palatable," was his only remark. Others had a great deal to say.

"We found the quality [of the food] on the whole bad," wrote William Robertson, another arrival from Scotland who traveled across the continent ten years before Stevenson. "All three meals . . . were almost identical, viz., tea, buffalo steaks, antelope chops, sweet potatoes, and boiled Indian corn, with hoe cakes and syrup *ad nauseam*." When supplies ran thin, a creative chef might serve up a heaping "chicken stew" made from prairie dog, rattlesnake, or armadillo.

On this sixth day out of New York, Stevenson's stomach began acting up again, so he chose to skip the combat of lunch altogether. Instead, he took a walk around the tiny town he found himself in, Cozad, Nebraska. A recent rain had left the dirt streets a quagmire of mud. Only a few skinny boards served as a sidewalk and saved him from sinking to his ankles in the brown goo. All the buildings—and there were only twelve of them lined up to face the tracks—were identical in size and shape and reminded Stevenson of shoe boxes. Surrounding the town and unbroken by any building or tree or mountain were flat grasslands.

*   *   *

Hundreds of towns like Cozad had come into existence during the construction of the transcontinental railroad. Wherever large numbers of workers were, a village of one-story wooden shacks would appear, sometimes overnight. Many of the

A view of Bear River City's main street in 1868. It's hard to tell from this picture, but at the time, over two hundred people called this town home. A few months after the track crews moved on, Bear River City vanished forever. (Union Pacific Museum Collection)

This panoramic view of Corinne, Utah, shows what a Hell on Wheels town looked like on a Sunday morning in 1868. At the time, Corinne was known as "the Chicago of the West." (Oakland Museum)

"buildings" were nothing more then big tents with wooden fronts added on to give them a feeling of permanence.

While a lot of everyday businesses lined the streets, such as stables, bakeries, and restaurants, the majority of buildings were either saloons or houses of prostitution. These were rough and rowdy towns, especially after the pay train arrived with workers' hard-earned dollars. Very few of these places had any sort of police or legal system, so personal protection and justice came in the form of a fist, knife, or handgun.

Of course, construction on the railroad never halted, and sooner or later, work crews would be too far away from town for their nightly visits. When this happened, enterprising businessmen took apart their buildings and had them shipped ahead by railroad flatcar to stay close to their patrons. These places could move so quickly and easily that they came to be referred to as Hell on Wheels.

16TH STREET CHEYENNE-1868

Most Hell on Wheels towns disappeared once the work crews moved down the tracks. Because Cheyenne was near traditional cattle routes, it managed to survive and prosper after the railroad was completed. (Union Pacific Museum Collection)

Many Hell on Wheels towns managed to survive after the work gangs and vice peddlers were gone. Yet even as these places grew quieter and more settled, their reputations for wickedness and violence lived on, thanks to the dime novels and guidebooks of the era.

One such very popular guidebook in the 1870s was H. Wallace Atwell's *The Great Trans-Continental Railroad Guide,* which he published under the pen name of "Bill Dadd, The Scribe." Atwell had never traveled farther west than Chicago, but that didn't stop him from describing the seedier aspects of places he hadn't visited in melodramatic detail. He cautioned first-time travelers that "thieves, gamblers, cut-throats and prostitutes stalked brazen-faced in broad day through the streets."

Atwell's book sold over a half million copies, and was probably passed around Stevenson's car during the long journey. This book, along with scores of other equally imaginative guidebooks and novels, helped sustain the idea that western towns were inhabited largely by devious, evil, and violent people, an image that persisted (due in large part to movies and television shows) well into the twentieth century.

* * *

Cozad didn't appear very violent to Stevenson as he tiptoed along the board sidewalks. In fact, it seemed so dull and isolated that he wondered how anyone could live in such a place. "What livelihood can repay a human creature for a life spent in this sameness? He is cut off from books, from news, from company. . . . A sky full of stars is the most varied spectacle that he can hope for. He may walk five miles and see nothing; ten, and it is as though he had not moved; twenty, and still he is in the midst of the same great level, and has approached no nearer to the one object in view, the flat horizon."

During his stroll, Stevenson came to a building where a woman was selling milk. "She was largely formed; her features were more than comely; she had that great rarity—a fine complexion which became her; and her eyes were kind, dark, and steady." What surprised Stevenson, however, wasn't her appearance. It was her manner. "She sold milk with patriarchal grace. There was not a line in her countenance, not a note in her soft and sleepy voice, but spoke of an entire contentment with her life. It would have been . . . arrogance to pity such a woman."

Her kindness made such a strong impression on Stevenson because "civility is the main comfort that you miss. Equality, though conceived very largely in America, does not extend so low down as to an emigrant."

In general, the train conductors never bothered to answer questions from the emigrants, not even those about the train schedule, and the newsboys were often rude, too. This lack of courtesy was also why Stevenson did not linger long over the glass of milk he had bought. While the standard practice on all trains carrying first- and second-class passengers was to announce the departure with a warning cry of *All aboard!* no such signal was given on emigrant trains. When the allotted twenty-minute dining time was up, the engineer simply opened the throttle and "the train stole from the station without a note of warning, and you had to keep an eye upon it even while you ate." This made boarding the train as much of a frantic rush as the initial departure; the only difference was

OPPOSITE: *This Pullman conductor has a steady, determined look about him. Once when Stevenson asked one of his conductors when their train would stop for dinner, the man refused to give any information because "one answer led to many other questions . . . and he could not afford to be eternally worried."* (Denver Public Library)

that many passengers entered the car clutching the remnants of their meals.

On Sunday, they entered the hilly terrain of the Rocky Mountains. Soon the train began climbing up some steep grades, the engine puffing and hissing loudly. Stevenson was eager for the change of scenery after traveling on flat land for over six hundred miles. "To cross such a plain is to grow home-sick for the mountains." If he hoped to see something beautiful, he was in for a shock.

"All Sunday and Monday we travelled through these sad mountains . . . tumbled boulders, cliffs that drearily imitate the shape of monuments and fortifications . . . not a tree, not a patch of [grass], not one shapely or commanding form; sage-brush, eternal sage-brush; over all, the same weariful and gloomy colouring, greys warming into brown, greys darkening towards black; and for sole sign of life, here and there a few fleeing antelope; here and there, but at incredible intervals, a creek running in a canyon."

Several things contributed to Stevenson's grumpy tone and his negative impression of the Rockies. First, the caring and kindness of the woman selling milk had reminded him of Fanny. He had not received any word about her health since New York, and the lack of news made him fear the very worst. Second, his own illness had worsened and, on top of that, he had developed a scratchy cough. "The hot weather and the fever put into my blood by so much continuous travel, had aggravated [my illness] till it was strangely difficult to bear. When the fit was on me, I grew almost light headed." And third, the railroad had not been built for sightseeing. The railroad's surveyors and engineers had chosen the quickest and easiest routes through the mountains because they would be the cheapest to build. No thought had been given to whether a route was scenic or not.

Both the Union and the Central Pacific hired skilled photographers to record the building of the transcontinental railroad and the scenery of the West. Here, J. B. Silvis's rolling photographic studio has stopped near Point of Rocks, Wyoming, in 1868. Silvis is in the center on the car platform. (Union Pacific Museum Collection)

Three Union Pacific engines and two cabooses have stopped on a recently constructed trestle at Devil's Gate, Utah, to test its ability to hold weight. (Union Pacific Museum Collection)

Stevenson wasn't alone in feeling sad and tired; the mood throughout the car had turned negative. The spirit of determination and adventure had sagged under the weight of day-and-night travel. Faces that once had seemed open and friendly were now blank and strained. Illness was common on emigrant trains because sanitary conditions were so poor, but Stevenson suspected another cause.

"As we continued to steam westward toward the land of gold, we were continually passing other emigrant trains upon the journey east; and these were as crowded as our own. Had all these return voyagers made a fortune? It would seem not, for, whenever we met them, the passengers ran to the platform and cried to us through the windows, in a kind of wailing chorus, to 'come back.' On the plains of Nebraska, in the mountains of Wyoming, it was still the same cry, and dismal to my heart, 'Come back!' "

The hardships of the West were growing more and more apparent. The travelers could see the rough, hostile terrain from their windows; at each stop they heard stories of droughts, swarms of grasshoppers devouring crops, and Indian attacks on isolated farms. The train tracks often ran alongside the old wagon route, where the bones of long-dead oxen and horses, solitary grave markers, broken wheels, and discarded furniture were a common sight. The easy life that the brochures had promised them was not to be had—not without hard work, sweat, and danger.

Stevenson began to worry about Fanny again and was unable to sleep at night. "The lamps did not go out; each made a faint shining in its own neighborhood, and the shadows were confounded together in the long, hollow box of the car. The sleepers lay in uneasy attitudes; here two chums alongside, flat upon their backs like dead folk; there a man sprawling on the floor, with his face upon his arm; there another half-seated with his head and shoulders on the bench."

Many of his travel companions groaned and murmured in their sleep, and now and then one would mutter a few half-formed words. The dreams that had brought them thousands of miles to a new land were now beginning to betray them as well.

Stevenson slid his window open a bit and breathed in the chill air. "Outside, in a glimmering night, I saw the black, amorphous hills shoot by unweariedly into our wake. They that long for morning have never longed for it more earnestly than I."

The Central Pacific emigrant car Stevenson boarded had more room, plus pull-down beds above the seats. While this 1885 picture was entitled "The Modern Ship of the Plains," the seats still look hard and very uncomfortable. (New-York Historical Society)

5

Across the High Sierras

THE NEXT MORNING, the train slid into Ogden, Utah, the last station on the Union Pacific's part of the transcontinental journey. A Central Pacific train would take them the rest of the way. For the third time, a very weary Stevenson collected his bags, books, bedding, and cooking utensils and boarded another emigrant car. Once again, he had to endure the time-consuming and bone-jangling operation of having one baggage car after another loaded and coupled to the train. It was a dry, hot day and Stevenson should have been miserable. Instead, he was in a remarkably happy mood.

Boarding a Central Pacific train meant he was nearing the end of his trip. Over eight hundred miles (and two more train transfers) still separated him from his beloved Fanny, but the stationmaster at Ogden told him he should be able to cover the distance in just a few days. What was more, the new emigrant car turned out to be surprisingly pleasant.

"The cars on the Central Pacific were nearly twice as high [as the Union Pacific cars] and so proportionally airier; they were freshly varnished, which gave us all a sense of cleanliness as though we had bathed; the seats drew out and joined in the

A Union Pacific work engine stops at Weber Canyon, Utah, in 1869, just long enough to let A. J. Russell photograph a recently erected trestle bridge. (Union Pacific Museum Collection)

centre, so that there was no need for bed-boards; and there was an upper tier of berths which could be closed by day and opened at night."

This may account for the unusually kind words he had for the railroad company. "In every way the accommodations [were] more cheerful and comfortable.... The company deserve our thanks. It was the first sign I could observe of any kindly purpose towards the emigrant."

Soon the train was rolling again, this time across the Great Salt Lake Desert. "We travelled all day through deserts of alkali and sand, horrible to man, and bare sage-brush country that seemed little kindlier."

There were the usual stops for fuel, water, and meals. At one tiny station in Nevada sitting on a bleak, high-lying plateau, the man who ran the eating house appeared at Stevenson's table. He had heard Stevenson's accent and came over to announce himself as a fellow Scot. After some chitchat, the man warned Stevenson about hostile Indians.

For Stevenson, this was old news. Ever since Chicago, he had heard such warnings and the lurid tales that went with them. (He had no way of knowing it, but most of these stories were either invented or wildly exaggerated by insurance agents eager to sell policies to worried settlers.) Stevenson had few encounters with Native Americans, noting that "they avoid the neighborhood of the train." In the Wyoming foothills, however, a Cheyenne family ventured onto the train platform, perhaps because they wanted to get a close look at the steaming, hissing locomotive and its human cargo. Whatever the family's reason for being there, the mother and father and two children were immediately surrounded by curious emigrants eager to meet "a real, live Indian." To Stevenson's disgust, curiosity soon turned to meanness when "my fellow-passengers danced and jested around them with [true] baseness."

Bad manners were one thing, but Stevenson realized something else. The continent they were all steaming across had once belonged to Native Americans. "If oppression drives a wise man mad, what should be raging in the hearts of these tribes, who have been driven back, step by step, their [land] torn from them . . . as the States extended westward, until at length they are shut up into these hideous mountain deserts of the centre—and even there find themselves invaded, insulted, and hunted out . . . ?"

*   *   *

"Hunted out" was the precise phrase for what had happened to Native Americans. When the federal government decided to back the construction of a transcontinental railroad and to allow the sale of millions of acres of western land, another, graver decision was also reached: Native Americans living on these lands would either accept the situation or be driven away by force.

Understandably, most Native Americans were extremely upset and angry when railroad representatives appeared on their ancestral lands to announce the coming of the railroad—and with it, hordes of settlers. Some tribes vowed to fight the trespassers to the end, and even attacked workers.

The railroads took the threats and violence seriously. The Central Pacific tried to head off trouble by signing a treaty with the Paiute and Shoshone that, ironically, paid them to help build the railroad and gave them free passes to travel on the trains. The federal government attempted to negotiate treaties with other tribes that pushed them onto undesirable bits of reservation land. Later, when gold or silver was discovered on these reservations, the government "renegotiated" the treaties and forced the tribes to move to even worse locations.

Silas Seymour, a Union Pacific engineer, put the matter very bluntly when he spoke before Congress in 1868. "It is in vain that these poor, ignorant creatures attempt to stay [the railroad's] progress by resisting inch by inch, and foot by foot, its onward march over these lovely plains, where but a few years since they were 'monarchs of all they surveyed.'

Being able to see real Native Americans was one of the tourist attractions of a train ride. Here, a Northern Pacific freight train has come to a halt so that riders can gawk at a small encampment of tepees. (DeGolyer Library)

Native Americans were rarely portrayed in a positive way. They were shown to be either meek and in awe of the white man's culture . . .
(Library of Congress)

... *or sneaky and underhanded, as in Jacob Gogolin's painting of warriors ripping up a section of track in order to derail a train. The former view suggested that, like innocent children, Native Americans needed close supervision and guidance; the latter gave backing to those who wished to exterminate them.* (Kansas State Historical Society)

"The locomotive must go forward until it reaches the Rocky Mountains, the Laramie Plains, the Great Salt Lake, the Sierra Nevada, and the Pacific Ocean. Lateral roads must also be built, extending in all directions from the main line, as veins from an artery, and penetrating the hunting-grounds of these worse than useless Indian tribes, until they are . . . driven from the face of the earth."

Many tribes, trusting in the white man's government and wanting to avoid violence, accepted treaty agreements and moved to the reservations (only to be betrayed later). Others, such as the Sioux and Cheyenne, resisted with all their might.

At first, railroads assumed most of the responsibility for their own defense. Workers kept rifles nearby in case of attack, and scouts and sharpshooters were hired to protect the men. Eventually, the railroads convinced President Ulysses S. Grant and Congress that federal troops were needed.

The officer appointed to bring the western tribes into line was General William T. Sherman. (Sherman's middle initial stood for Tecumseh, the name of the great Shawnee leader. Sherman took no pride in it and never spelled it out fully when signing his name.) Sherman had fought in the Civil War and had become famous for his brutal march through Georgia and South Carolina. During that campaign everything his army encountered was destroyed—factories, railroads, bridges, homes, churches, and farms. Commenting on the severity of his tactics, his explanation was simple: "We are not only fighting hostile armies, but a hostile people, and must make old and young, rich and poor, feel the hard hand of war."

Sherman carried this philosophy into his handling of the belligerent tribes. "We must act with vindictive earnestness against [them], even to their extermination, men, women, and children."

To carry out his orders, Sherman had the help of another

Civil War veteran, General Philip H. Sheridan. Sheridan shared his boss's thinking about how to handle the tribes, as well as his disdain for them. He said, "The Indian is a lazy, idle vagabond. He never labors, and has no profession except that of arms, to which he is raised from a child; a scalp is constantly dangled before his eyes, and the highest honor he can aspire to is to possess one taken by himself."

Not all people agreed with this portrayal of Native Americans or with the way their government was treating them. Even the army commander Colonel Henry B. Carrington was repulsed by what was happening. "There never was a more ill-considered impulse of the American people than that which forced the army . . . to serve the behests of irresponsible speculative emigration, regardless of the rights of the tribes rightfully in possession."

Unfortunately, these voices of protest were neither strong enough nor united enough to be very effective. Popular opinion weighed heavily in favor of military action and Sherman's view of how to handle it: "The more we can kill this year, the less will have to be killed the next . . . for the more I see of these Indians the more convinced I am that they all have to be killed."

Numerous battles would be fought over the next three decades. Native American warriors managed to win a few of these, most notably at Little Big Horn, but for the most part they lacked the supplies and firepower to defeat the federal army. Meanwhile, Native Americans confined to reservations suffered and starved as bison herds were decimated and promised food was never delivered. There were approximately one million Native Americans living at the beginning of the seventeenth century; by 1900, their numbers had been reduced to about three hundred thousand.

The genocide of Native Americans was in full swing when

Some Native Americans did resist the invasion and seizure of their lands, but with little success. This picture shows the legendary Geronimo (front row, third from the right) and members of his tribe under arrest after a failed rebellion. The machine that has brought so many unwanted white settlers to their land is taking them to a detention camp in Florida. (Smithsonian Institution)

Stevenson traveled in the West and, while he never saw any actual violence, he recoiled at the idea. "The eviction of the [tribes], the extortion of Indian agents, the outrages of the wicked, the ill-faith of all, nay, down to the ridicule of such poor beings [by those] here with me upon the train, make up a chapter of injustice and indignity such as a man must be . . . base if his heart will suffer him to pardon or forget."

*　*　*

To Stevenson's relief, the small family on that Wyoming platform were saved further insults when the train pulled out of

Only a few years before, the land was home to one million Native Americans. Now a band of steel cuts the terrain in half, signaling the growth of one culture and the decline of another. (Society of California Pioneers)

The old way of travel meets the new near the Great Salt Lake, Utah. Such meetings were somewhat common and allowed for the exchange of news and passengers. (New-York Historical Society)

the station and their tormentors had to scramble aboard or be left behind. The train went around a long curve, and Stevenson, peering back through the window, saw that the Cheyennes were still standing on the platform, talking among themselves. "The silent stoicism of their conduct . . . would have touched any thinking person. I was ashamed for the thing we call civilization."

The train slid through Nevada, canyon after winding canyon. Stevenson's cough persisted and made sleeping difficult. He distracted himself by reading Bancroft's history. "Of all the next day I will tell you nothing," he wrote, "for the best of all reasons, that I remember no more than that we continued through desolate and desert scenes, fiery hot and deadly weary."

It was in the afternoon of the eleventh day that the train

came to the foot of the Sierra Nevada mountain range and began its slow climb. Many of the mountain grades were so steep that two and sometimes three engines had to be joined together to haul up the long train. The steep angle of the grade pinned passengers back in their seats and made moving very difficult. The wall of cracked, jagged rock on one side of the car blocked out the light, creating an eerie gloom. On the other side, the ground dropped away, sometimes for hundreds of feet. A buzz ran through the cars as stories of failed brakes and faulty bridge construction were recalled.

Two engines huff and puff as they haul a string of baggage and passenger cars into the rocky Sierras. (Denver Public Library)

If Stevenson was alarmed, he did not mention it. He spent the hours reading his *History of the United States* and dozing. It was only when the train came to a flat stretch that Stevenson took notice of his surroundings. "I was puzzled for a while to know if it were day or night, for the illumination was unusual. I sat up at last, and found we were grading slowly through a long snowshed."

*   *   *

During the building of this section of the railroad, snowstorms had often held up tracklaying for days and weeks at a time. Not only was it impossible for the men to work, but twenty- and thirty-foot snowdrifts stopped supply trains from running on the track already completed. To keep work moving forward, the Central Pacific had thirty-seven miles of wooden sheds erected in the places where the snow was deepest.

These were impressive structures. The beams were massive, twelve inches wide and twenty-four inches deep, and the walls soared twenty-five feet into the air to allow the tall engine stacks to pass through. In addition to covering the tracks, sheds were constructed to protect a number of stations as well as the homes of the station crews.

Children grew up inside these great wooden caverns, playing in the strange dim light while the wind outside tugged and whistled through cracks in the walls. They also lived with the constant fear of fire. Sparks from a locomotive stack sometimes set sections of the shed on fire, and it would soon fill up with choking smoke. To combat fires, railroad companies stationed men every mile or so with buckets of water.

On track outside the sheds, snow was still a problem. In December 1872, three hundred fifty passengers were snowbound between Percy and Cheyenne for over two weeks. By

To keep trains moving through the Sierras, the Central Pacific built snowsheds in places where the snow tended to drift very high. (Author's collection)

Standing firewatch inside a snowshed could be a very lonely job. (George Eastman House)

the time help reached them, passengers had resorted to burning parts of the train to stay warm and to melting ice for water.

If a train couldn't get through a drift, it wasn't unusual for the engineer to order everyone outside to help with the shoveling. With bigger drifts, the engineer might try "bucking the

One way to free the train was to have the crew and passengers shovel the tracks clear. If this failed, an engineer could try ramming his way through. (Museum of the City of New York)

snow." The train was backed away from the drift and the engine would be uncoupled from the cars. Then the engine would ram the snow several times in an attempt to break through to clear track.

Eventually, effective snowplows were designed and the

But sometimes the snow won the battle. Here, three engines have stalled in deep snow outside Wisconsin Dells, Wisconsin. (State Historical Society of Wisconsin)

snows became less of a problem. Dismantling the sheds would cost millions of dollars, so instead, the Central Pacific decided to do nothing. Over the years, the sheds deteriorated and fell down; when fires started, they were allowed to burn unchecked. In time, this unusual aspect of a transcontinental train trip disappeared forever.

* * *

Almost the entire length of snowsheds was still intact when Stevenson crossed the Sierras. The railroad company had made one concession to passengers: to relieve the miles of darkness, and to afford a glimpse of the passing scenery, it had thousands of large, rectangular sections cut out of the sides of the sheds. Looking through these cutouts was like blinking one's eyes hundreds of times in a row, a dizzying thing for healthy travelers. For someone like Stevenson, who was not in the best of health, it was undoubtedly worse. This portion of the trip must have made Stevenson's head swim and his stomach lurch. His only medicine was the solitude of sleep.

"But some time after I had fallen asleep that night, I was awakened by one of my companions. It was in vain that I resisted. The fire of enthusiasm and whisky burned in his eyes; and he declared we were in a new country, and I must come forth upon the platform and see with my own eyes."

During Stevenson's fitful sleep and while still inside the snowsheds, the train had stopped at Summit Station at the very top of the mountain to take on fuel and water. One mile after beginning the descent on the western side of the Sierras, the snowsheds ended, and the train entered a secluded valley where it pulled to the side to let another express train go past.

"[Our] train was then, in its patient way, standing halted in a by-track. It was a clear, moonlit night; but the valley was too

A train rounds a curve high in the mountains. Two brakemen stand on top of the cars taking in the scene. (Society of California Pioneers)

This train has paused momentarily at a scenic spot to allow passengers a good look. (Society of California Pioneers)

narrow to admit the moonshine direct, and only a diffused glimmer whitened the tall rocks and relieved the blackness of the pines. A hoarse clamour filled the air; it was the continuous plunge of a cascade somewhere near at hand among the mountains. The air struck chill, but tasted good and vigorous in the nostrils—a fine, dry, old mountain atmosphere. I was dead sleepy, but I returned to roost with a grateful mountain feeling in my heart."

The heights in the Sierras could be dizzying at times. A passenger train rumbles across a frail-looking wooden trestle hundreds of feet above the rocks and water. The workers at the base of the trestle are checking to make sure winter snows and spring flooding haven't weakened the structure. (New-York Historical Society)

6

In the Good Country

FROM THE SUMMIT STATION ON, the journey was literally all downhill. In fact, during the 105 miles from the top of the Sierras to Sacramento, California, the railroad tracks dropped almost seven thousand feet. The downward grade was so steep and steady that for nearly fifty miles of the descent the train coasted along without the aid of steam.

Some riders found this silent, twisting ride unnerving. This was especially true when the train shot out onto a bridge hundreds of feet high and the ground around them dropped away. For Stevenson, the change of scenery seemed to overcome any fear he might have felt. "I had a glimpse of a huge pine-forested ravine upon my left, a foaming river, and a sky already coloured with the fires of dawn. I am usually very calm over the displays of nature; but you will scarce believe how my heart leaped at this. . . . [It was as though] I had come home again—home from unsightly deserts to the green and hospitable corners of the earth. Every spire of pine along the hilltop, every trouty pool along the mountain river, was more dear to me than a blood-relation."

What Stevenson and his fellow travelers didn't realize was

The train has stopped to allow the crew and passengers to peer over the cliff at Cape Horn. (New-York Historical Society)

that the engineer was no longer in full control of the train. On the long downhill sections, the train and the lives of everyone on board were in the hands of the brakemen. Perched on top of the cars, the brakemen were struggling to control the speed of the train by applying the brakes. Several years before Stevenson's trip, an Englishman named William Rae had come down the mountainside at night and been petrified by the experience. "The velocity with which the train rushed down this incline, and the suddenness with which it wheeled around curves, produced a sensation which cannot be reproduced in words.... The axle boxes smoked with the friction and the odour of burning wood pervaded the cars. The wheels were

A brakeman struggles to turn the brake wheel despite an icy snow and freezing fingers. (Author's collection)

The Central Pacific section of the transcontinental railroad was built almost completely by Chinese laborers brought over from their homeland. Few close-up photos exist of the Chinese workers. Some historians claim that they were shy and refused to pose for photographs; a more likely explanation is that the Central Pacific was not eager to publicize the fact that nonwhite workers were the chief muscle power behind the construction of an American railroad. Here tracklayers have stopped long enough for J. B. Silvis to take this photo in 1869. (Denver Public Library)

nearly red hot. In the darkness of the night they resembled discs of fire."

The most dangerous section of track was at Cape Horn, where the twists and dips resembled those of a roller coaster. Guidebooks suggested that the very timid and those with weak hearts might want to avert their eyes rather than look down into the gorge two thousand feet below. One of the first travelers on the transcontinental railroad, William Humason, remembered Cape Horn vividly: "We follow the track around the sides of high mountains, looking down into a canyon of awful depth, winding around for miles, until we almost meet the track we have before been over—so near that one would think we could almost throw a stone across."

* * *

When the train was at the very lip of these cliffs, it's possible that Stevenson thought about the men who had cut the tortuous route out of the stone. It was the building of the Central Pacific's section of the transcontinental railroad that started another great wave of emigration to this country.

As the Union Pacific crews worked their way westward, tracklaying for the Central Pacific had stalled just outside Sacramento. It seemed that every time a new gold or silver strike was announced, railroad laborers (mostly Irish) grabbed their picks and shovels and headed for the hills.

Finally, out of desperation, the Central Pacific hired fifty Chinese laborers in 1865. Initially, the Chinese were given the very easy chore of filling the horse-drawn dump carts with rock debris and driving them away. They performed this task effortlessly and were "promoted" to the task of clearing rock from the path for the roadbed. Before long, the Chinese were also doing the more skilled jobs of masonry, tracklaying, and using explosives.

Of course, fifty men by themselves could not build a railroad. The Central Pacific needed five thousand workers, and to find them it sent recruiting agents throughout the United States, and, eventually, to China. To induce poor individuals, the railroad offered to lend potential workers the twenty-five dollars needed to sail across the Pacific.

In just a few months, tracklaying was once again moving along at the mile-a-day pace expected. Despite the Chinese workers' obvious skill, many people still doubted their ability to endure the brutal work. They seemed thin and frail compared to the brawny, tough men usually employed for such labor. Then construction came to a dead halt at Cape Horn.

No one had ever attempted to lay track along such a fearsome cliff, and the white foreman of the work crews wasn't sure how to attack the job. It was the Chinese workers who came up with the solution, based on similar construction in the Yangtze Valley.

First, they used reeds brought from San Francisco to weave waist-high baskets, each large enough to hold one man. A Chinese worker would climb into a basket and be lowered by rope to a position on the rock wall. There, the worker chipped away and drilled at the wall until he could insert a charge of explosives. Then he would light the charge and scramble up the rope as quickly as possible before the explosion ripped a gaping hole in the rock.

Slowly, painfully, ridges were blasted out of the side of the cliff, then widened and made ready for the rails. Three hundred men labored on the wall for ten days, managing to cut away about one mile of rock. Sometimes a man, exhausted

OPPOSITE: *The terrain in the Sierras was breathtakingly beautiful and wildly irregular. Whenever a hill seemed too steep, Chinese workers brought in tons of dirt to create a level roadbed. All of the work was done by hand.* (Huntington Library)

The finishing touches are being made to the Secrettown Trestle.
(Huntington Library)

from drilling the rock, was slow in climbing the rope and the blast carried him off. On several occasions the rope snapped and sent the worker plunging to his death. And still, the work went on until the tracks had rounded Cape Horn.

"The rugged mountains looked like stupendous anthills," a travel writer reported to his readers. "They swarm with [Chinese] shoveling, wheeling, carting, drilling and blasting rocks and earth."

After Cape Horn, the Chinese workers punched eighteen tunnels through sheer granite, each at least a thousand feet long. They brought the track down the eastern slope of the Sierras during some of the worst snowstorms, erecting thirty-seven miles of snowsheds along the way, then pushed across the desert, where they set the record of ten miles of track laid in a single day. (Some historians have speculated that, in addition to an amazing work ethic, a part of the secret behind the stamina and strength of the Chinese was their diet. It was made up largely of vegetables, with only a little meat; white workers ate much heavier meals of beef or bison, beans, bread, butter, and potatoes, all washed down with beer.) For their incredible effort, Chinese workers were paid less than white workers—about one dollar a day, plus tea and meals of food imported from China.

Instead of earning respect for their achievements, the Chinese were scorned and ridiculed. Many whites feared the Chinese would steal their jobs away or thought they were stupid because they spoke English with an accent. Even their daily habits were considered odd or threatening. Stevenson recalled that the Chinese were made fun of because they washed their bodies, even their feet, every day, while the white passengers "pigged and stewed in one infamy, [and only] wet our hands and faces for half a minute daily . . . and were unashamed."

Chinese workers were paid less than white workers, but they were given a few special benefits. One of them was a tea break. This tea carrier has stopped just outside the mouth of an unfinished tunnel. (Colorado Historical Society)

After the railroad was completed, most of the Central Pacific's five thousand Chinese workers stayed in America, establishing strong communities in a number of cities. This festive dragon is wandering down the main street of Rock Springs, Wyoming, in 1899, as a part of the Chinese New Year celebration. (Colorado Historical Society)

A few of the Chinese laborers would gather up their hard-earned savings and return to China when the transcontinental railroad was completed. Most stayed and signed on with other railroad companies, which were beginning work on their own western routes. The rest took the train back to San Francisco or established communities in large cities such as Chicago and New York.

Few people realized or cared that the Central Pacific section of the transcontinental railroad would never have been completed on time without the Chinese. In the same year that Stevenson traveled, the Workingman's Party of California pushed through a law that prohibited companies in California from hiring Chinese workers. In 1882, the party convinced the federal government to suspend admission of all Asian emigrants for ten years.

The leader of the Workingman's Party was an Irishman named Denis Kearney, who had left Ireland with his family when he was a young boy. Stevenson found the situation sadly ironic. Kearney and other Irish immigrants, who had once faced the same prejudice and hate, were now passing it on to another group of arrivals. "A while ago it was the Irish," Stevenson said, "now it is the Chinese that must go. Such is the cry. It seems, after all, that no country is bound to submit to immigration any more than to invasion."

Such thoughts troubled Stevenson a great deal during his journey. The United States was a land noted for freedom, and yet he saw all around him people who were targets of prejudice—Native Americans, Chinese, blacks, and many of his fellow emigrants. Stevenson had even found people suspicious of him because of his thick Scottish accent.

*   *   *

The only relief Stevenson had from such sad recollections was the fact that every inch he traveled brought him that much closer to Fanny. His tone during the rapid descent after Cape Horn is almost giddy. "Down by Blue Cañon, Alta, Dutch Flat, and all the old mining camps, through a sea of mountain forests, dropping thousands of feet toward the far sea-level as we went, not I only, but all the passengers on board, threw off their sense of dirt and heat and weariness, and bawled like schoolboys."

Many of the passengers, including Stevenson, crowded onto the car's observation platform to drink in the fresh, sweet air and to see the sights. "The sun no longer oppressed us with heat, it only shone laughingly along the mountain-side, until we were fain to laugh ourselves for glee. At every turn we could see farther into the land and our own futures."

Even though the distance from Summit Station to the Sacramento Valley was only a little over a hundred miles on the map, the hundreds of twists and turns seemed to triple the distance. Then suddenly, the land began to level out and the train chugged across the floor of the valley.

The change was complete and dramatic. The mountain cliffs and towering trees that blocked the view disappeared; the sky opened up, wide and brilliantly blue, while the sun warmed the air. At first passengers saw cattle grazing on rolling grasslands, but this soon changed to fields of corn and wheat, broken in many places by orchards. Solidly built houses surrounded by shade trees and flowers dotted the countryside and seemed familiar and welcoming. The train paused briefly in Sacramento, then steamed on rapidly. "By afternoon we were in Sacramento, the city of gardens in a plain of corn; and the next day before dawn we were lying-to upon the Oakland side of San Francisco Bay."

Stevenson wasted no time at all. He had no idea whether Fanny was alive or not, but wired ahead anyway to say he was coming. A ferry ride took him to San Francisco, where he boarded the very next train out. Between San Francisco and Monterey there would be one more switch of trains—the fifth time he had done this in twelve days.

He stumbled off the train in Monterey, baggage and books in hand, looking very much like a skeleton—bent over and frail, his cheeks sunken, his skin sallow and pale. Every few steps he stopped to cough and catch his breath. Later, Fanny's eleven-year-old son, Lloyd, would recall, "He looked ill even to my childish eyes. . . . His clothes, no longer picturesque but merely shabby, hung loosely on his shrunken body; there was about him an indescribable lessening of his alertness and self-confidence."

Nothing was going to stop Stevenson at this point in his journey, however. He summoned up every ounce of energy he had left and hired a horse-drawn carriage to take him to Fanny's house, where a lively and emotional reunion took place. "I remember him walking into the room," said Lloyd, "and the outcry of delight that greeted him, the incoherence, the laughter, the tears; the heart-welling joy of reunion."

After the initial celebration calmed down, Stevenson must have been pleasantly surprised when he took a really good look at Fanny. Instead of an invalid suffering from brain fever, he was looking at the same energetic and animated person he had last seen in France over a year ago. In the twenty-four days it had taken him to travel from Scotland to Monterey, she had managed a full recovery. As it turned out, Stevenson was the one who would need careful nursing in order to regain his strength.

Stevenson and Fanny would make a number of trips to San

Francisco, but it's likely that he remembered his first sight of the area most vividly. He had traveled over three thousand miles across the tossing Atlantic, then endured another three thousand miles of dust and smoke and swaying passenger cars.

"The day was breaking as we crossed [on] the ferry [from Oakland]; the fog was rising over the citied hills of San Francisco; the bay was perfect—not a ripple, scarce a stain, upon its blue expanse; everything was waiting, breathless, for the sun. A spot of cloudy gold lit first upon the head of [Mount] Tamalpais, and then widened downward on its shapely shoulder; the air seemed to awaken, and began to sparkle; and suddenly . . . the city of San Francisco, and the bay of gold and corn, were lit from end to end with summer daylight."

He and Fanny were together and his journey was truly complete. "For this was indeed our destination; this was 'the good country' we had been going to so long."

This drawing of Fanny is based on a photograph taken around the time she met Robert.

A Final Word

---◈---

THE GRUELING JOURNEY from Scotland to California had broken Stevenson's health. Fanny tried to convince him to rest as much as possible, and he followed her suggestions, but only to a point. Whenever he regained some of his strength, he would push himself out of bed and act as if he were in perfect health. Painfully aware of his poverty, Stevenson spent long hours at his writing, sometimes working through the night. When he wasn't writing, he went for hikes in the steep hills of Monterey and talked to the people living there (who were mostly poor Mexicans).

Fanny filed for and was granted a divorce early in 1880. On May 19 of that year, Fanny and Stevenson were married. Afterward, the happy couple, along with Fanny's children, honeymooned in Calistoga, California, a town renowned for its healing climate and hot springs.

Stevenson's health gradually improved, and he produced three short books (*The Amateur Emigrant* and *Across the Plains*, both about his recent journey, and *The Silverado Squatters*, about an abandoned mining town in the hills above Calistoga), as well as a number of short stories. In addition to reading her husband's manuscripts and offering strong editorial advice, Fanny launched a letter-writing campaign to win the approval of Stevenson's parents. She eventually succeeded through her directness and humor.

Many other things had changed for Stevenson, too. During his journey, he had not just seen poverty and discrimination, he had experienced them firsthand. This gave his writing a deeper, more mature feeling, especially when he wrote about the poor and their living conditions. He also picked up the cadences of everyday speech patterns from his fellow travelers, which resulted in a simpler and more accessible writing style.

Even the months he spent trying to regain his health had an effect on his writing. Many of the people he met in California found their way into his books, and his journal descriptions of the rugged Monterey coastline turn up in his novels about the sea.

Stevenson was paid one hundred pounds for the publication rights to *Treasure Island,* which appeared in 1884. It turned out to be his first real hit and was quickly followed by others, such as *The Black Arrow, A Child's Garden of Verses, Kidnapped, New Arabian Nights,* and *The Strange Case of Dr. Jekyll and Mr. Hyde.* The fame and fortune that had eluded him so long came to him in an amazing rush.

Sadly, Stevenson had little time to enjoy either his new family or his new success. His journey to be with the woman he loved had damaged his health more than he or anyone else imagined. The cough that developed during his train ride turned out to be the first sign of tuberculosis. He would suffer from respiratory problems and weakness for the rest of his life. He died in 1894 at the age of forty-four.

Through the many years his illness lasted, Stevenson refused to give in to it. He and Fanny traveled extensively, visiting Switzerland, Scotland, England, and France, then heading back to America. They would eventually sail to Australia and then settle for a while on the island of Samoa. During all of this time, Stevenson wrote constantly, even when fatigue overtook him. And he never once regretted his decision to leave Scotland and cross America on the emigrant train.

Stevenson could not afford to buy a gift for Fanny when they married, but he gave her something she cherished even more —a small collection of his poems. One of them contains these lines, and may very well have been written during his long train ride:

> *Hope is so strong that it has conquered fear;*
>   *Love follows, crowned and glad for fear's defeat.*
> *Down the long future I behold us, sweet,*
>   *Pass and grow ever dearer and more dear.*

Bibliography

One of the great pleasures about writing *Across America on an Emigrant Train* was doing research for the text and illustrations. I visited numerous libraries and museums and consulted hundreds of books, magazines, and newspapers. What follows is a very select bibliography of my source material. A number of the items have been long out of print or were privately published and are hard to find. I've included them because these are excellent firsthand accounts of nineteenth-century transcontinental train rides, and some libraries might have them in their special collections. Almost all libraries have a solid collection of railroad books, including oversize and sumptuously illustrated ones.

For those who want to see and maybe even ride a real steam passenger train, special mention has to be made of one book: *The Steam Passenger Service Directory* (published by Locomotive and Railway Preservation, Box 599, Richmond, Virginia 05477). This guide covers both the United States and Canada and has over three hundred listings for tourist-railroad, trolley, and railway-museum operations with regularly scheduled passenger service.

Enjoy your reading—and riding.

Adams, Alexander B. *Sitting Bull, an Epic of the Plains.* New York: G. P. Putnam's Sons, 1973.

Alexander, Edwin P. *Iron Horses: American Locomotives 1829–1900.* New York: Bonanza Books, 1941.

American Social Science Association. *Handbook for Immigrants to the United States.* Cambridge, Mass.: Riverside Press, 1871.

Atwell, H. Wallace. *The Great Transcontinental Railroad Guide.* Chicago: G. A. Crofutt & Co., 1869.

Bailey, W. F. *The Story of the First Trans-continental Railroad.* Pittsburgh: Pittsburgh Printing Co., 1906.

Barnes, Demas. *From the Atlantic to the Pacific, Overland.* New York: D. Van Nostrand Co., 1886.

Beadle, John Hanson. *The Undeveloped West.* Philadelphia: National Publishing Co., 1873.

Beebe, Lucius. *Highball.* New York: D. Appleton-Century Co., 1945.

Beebe, Lucius, and Charles Clegg. *Hear the Train Blow.* New York: E. P. Dutton & Co., 1952.

Berkeley, Grantley F. *The English Sportsman in the Western Prairies.* London: Hurst & Blackett, 1861.

Bowles, Samuel. *Our New West: Records of Travel Between the Mississippi River and the Pacific Ocean.* Hartford: Hartford Publishing Co., 1869.

———. *The Pacific Railroad—Open; How to Go; What to See.* Boston: Fields, Osgood & Co., 1869.

Clarke, Thomas C. *The American Railway.* New York: Charles Scribner's Sons, 1889.

Combs, Barry B. *Westward to Promontory.* Palo Alto: American West Publishing Co., 1969.

Connell, Evan S. *Son of the Morning Star: Custer and the Little Big-horn.* New York: HarperCollins, 1991.

Coolidge, Mary Roberts. *Chinese Immigration.* New York: Henry Holt & Co., 1909.

Coolidge, Susan. "A Few Hints on the California Journey." *The Century Magazine,* vol. VI (1873).

Crofutt, George A. *Crofutt's Trans-Continental Tourist's Guide.* Chicago: G. A. Crofutt & Co., 1871.

Davis, Richard Harding. *The West from a Car Window.* New York: Harper & Brothers, 1892.

Dodge, Grenville M. *How We Built the Union Pacific Railroad.* Ann Arbor: University Microfilms, 1966.

Drury, George H. *The Historical Guide to North American Railroads.* Milwaukee: Kalmbach Publishing Co., 1985.

Fisher, Leonard Everett. *Tracks Across America: The Story of the American Railroad 1825–1900.* New York: Holiday House, 1992.

Foreman, Grant. *The Last Trek of the Indians.* Chicago: University of Chicago Press, 1946.

Freedman, Russell. *Buffalo Hunt.* New York: Scholastic, 1988.

Furnas, J. C. *Voyage to Windward: The Life of Robert Louis Stevenson.* New York: William Sloane Associates, 1951.

Gibson, Rev. O. *The Chinese in America.* Cincinnati: Hitchcock & Walden, 1877.

Goddard, Fred B. *Union Pacific: Where to Emigrate and Why.* New York: Union Pacific Railroad Co., 1869.

Grinnell, George B. *The Fighting Cheyennes.* Norman: University of Oklahoma Press, 1956.

Griswold, Wesley S. *Train Wreck!* Brattleboro: The Stephen Greene Press, 1969.

———. *A Work of Giants: Building the First Transcontinental Railroad*. New York: McGraw-Hill, 1962.

Hardy, Lady Duffus. *Through Cities and Prairie Lands, Sketches of an American Tour*. New York: Worthington, 1890.

Harter, Jim. *Transportation: A Pictorial Archive from Nineteenth-Century Sources*. New York: Dover Publications, 1983.

Hinkley, Kaura L. *The Stevensons: Louis and Fanny*. New York: Hastings House, 1950.

Holbrook, Stewart H. *The Story of American Railroads*. New York: Crown Publishers, 1947.

Howard, Robert West. *The Great Iron Trail: The Story of the First Transcontinental Railroad*. New York: G. P. Putnam's Sons, 1962.

Hoyt, A. W. "Over the Plains to Colorado." *Harper's New Monthly Magazine* (June 1867).

Humason, William Lawrence. *From the Atlantic Surf to the Golden Gate*. Hartford: Press of Wm. C. Hutchings, 1869.

Husband, Joseph. *The Story of the Pullman Car*. Chicago: A. C. McClurg & Co., 1917.

Jackson, William Henry. *Time Exposure*. New York: G. P. Putnam's Sons, 1940.

Jackson, William Henry, and Howard R. Driggs. *The Pioneer Photographer*. Yonkers-on-Hudson, N.Y.: World Book Co., 1929.

Jensen, Oliver. *Railroads in America*. New York: American Heritage Publishing Co., 1975.

Knight, Oliver. *Following the Indian Wars: The Story of the Newspaper Correspondents Among the Indian Campaigners*. Norman: University of Oklahoma Press, 1960.

Leland, Charles G. *The Union Pacific Railway, Eastern Division or Three Thousand Miles in a Railway Car.* Philadelphia: Ringwalt & Brown, 1867.

Leonard, Levi O., and Jack T. Johnson. *A Railroad to the Sea.* Iowa City: Midland House, 1937.

Leslie, Mrs. Frank. *California, a Pleasure Trip from Gotham to the Golden Gate.* New York: Frank Leslie Publications, 1877.

Lester, John E. *The Atlantic to the Pacific, What to See, and How to See It.* Boston: Sheperd & Gill, 1873.

Lewis, Oscar. *The Big Four.* New York: Alfred A. Knopf, 1938.

Mackay, Margaret. *The Violent Friend: The Story of Mrs. Robert Louis Stevenson.* Garden City, N.Y.: Doubleday & Co., 1968.

McLeod, Alexander. *Pigtails and Gold Dust.* Caldwell, Iowa: The Caxton Printers, 1947.

Mencken, August. *The Railroad Passenger Car.* Baltimore: The Johns Hopkins Press, 1957.

Moody, John. *The Railroad Builders.* New Haven: Yale University Press, 1920.

O'Connor, Richard. *Iron Wheels and Broken Men.* New York: G. P. Putnam's Sons, 1973.

Rae, William F. *Westward by Rail: The New Route to the East.* New York: Appleton, 1871.

Reed, Robert C. *Train Wrecks.* New York: Bonanza Books, 1968.

Richardson, Albert D. *Beyond the Mississippi.* Hartford: American Publishing Co., 1867.

Robertson, Archie. *Slow Train to Yesterday.* Boston: Houghton Mifflin Co., 1945.

Robertson, William T., and W. F. Robertson. *Our American Tour: Being a Run of Ten Thousand Miles from the Atlantic to the Golden Gate, in the Autumn of 1869.* Edinburgh: W. Burness, 1871.

Russell, A. J. *The Great West Illustrated in a Series of Photographic Views Across the Continent; Taken Along the Line of the Union Pacific Railroad, West from Omaha, Nebraska.* Vol. 1. New York: Union Pacific Railroad Co., 1869.

Seymour, Silas. *Incidents of a Trip Through the Great Platte Valley to the Rocky Mountains and Laramie Plains in the Fall of 1866.* New York: D. Van Nostrand Co., 1867.

Smith, E. Boyd. *The Railroad Book.* Boston: Houghton Mifflin Co., 1913.

Stevenson, Robert Louis. *Across the Plains.* London: Chatto & Windus, 1892.

Stilgoe, John R. *Borderland: Origins of the American Suburb, 1820–1939.* New Haven: Yale University Press, 1988.

———. *Metropolitan Corridor: Railroads and the American Scene.* New Haven: Yale University Press, 1983.

Stover, John F. *American Railroads.* Chicago: University of Chicago Press, 1961.

Tilden, Freeman. *Following the Frontier with F. Jay Haynes.* New York: Alfred A. Knopf, 1964.

Wheeler, Keith. *The Railroaders.* New York: Time-Life Books, 1973.

White, John H. *The American Railroad Passenger Car.* Parts 1 and 2. Baltimore: The Johns Hopkins University Press, 1978.

White, Lonnie J. "Indian Raids on the Kansas Frontier, 1869." *Kansas Historical Quarterly,* vol. 38 (1972), 369–88.

Williams, Henry T. *The Pacific Tourist.* New York: Williams, 1879.

Index

Page numbers in *italics* refer to illustrations.

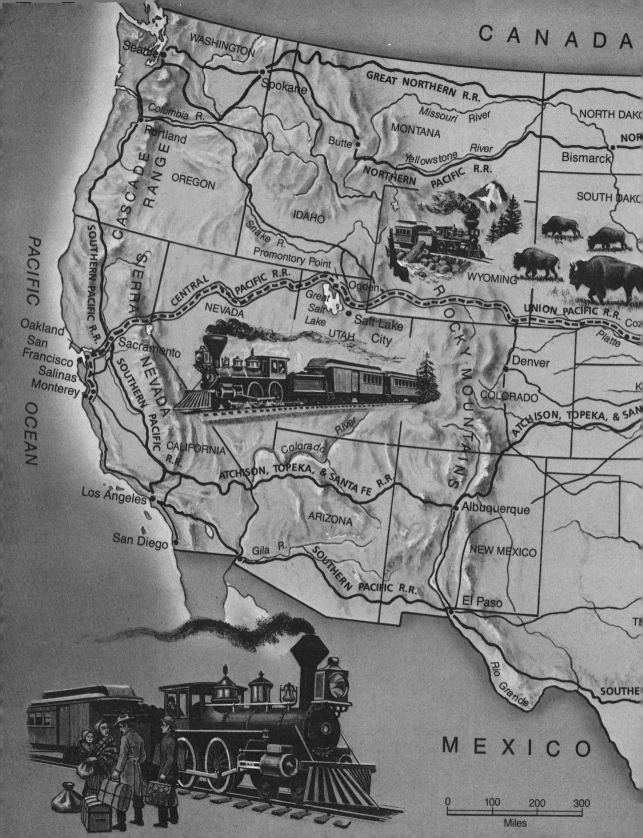

CANADA

WASHINGTON

Seattle

Spokane

GREAT NORTHERN R.R.

Columbia R.

Missouri River

NORTH DAK

Portland

Butte

MONTANA

NOR

Bismarck

CASCADE RANGE

OREGON

Yellowstone River

SOUTH DAKO

IDAHO

NORTHERN PACIFIC R.R.

Snake R.

Promontory Point

WYOMING

CENTRAL PACIFIC R.R.

Ogden

SOUTHERN PACIFIC R.R.

NEVADA

Great Salt Lake

Salt Lake City

ROCKY MOUNTAINS

UNION PACIFIC R.R.

Co

PACIFIC

Oakland
San Francisco
Salinas
Monterey

Sacramento

SIERRA NEVADA

UTAH

Platte

Denver

COLORADO

K

SOUTHERN PACIFIC

OCEAN

CALIFORNIA R.R.

Colorado River

ATCHISON, TOPEKA, & SAN

Los Angeles

ATCHISON, TOPEKA, & SANTA FE R.R.

San Diego

ARIZONA

Albuquerque

Gila R.

NEW MEXICO

SOUTHERN PACIFIC R.R.

El Paso

SOUTHE

Rio Grande

MEXICO

0   100   200   300

Miles

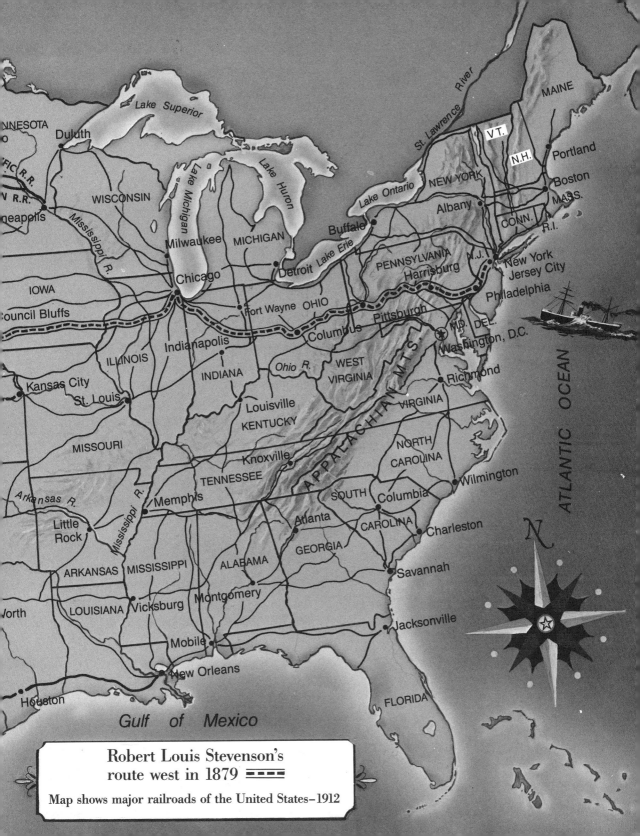

Lake Superior

NNESOTA
O
Duluth

PACIFIC R.R.
W R.R.
neapolis

Mississippi R.

WISCONSIN

Lake Michigan

Lake Huron

MICHIGAN

Milwaukee

Chicago

Detroit
Lake Erie

Buffalo

St. Lawrence River

MAINE

VT.

N.H.

Portland

Lake Ontario

NEW YORK

Albany

Boston

MASS.

CONN.

R.I.

PENNSYLVANIA

Harrisburg

N.J.

New York
Jersey City

Philadelphia

ATLANTIC OCEAN

IOWA

Council Bluffs

Fort Wayne
OHIO

Columbus

Pittsburgh

MD.
DEL.

Washington, D.C.

Indianapolis

ILLINOIS

INDIANA

Ohio R.

WEST
VIRGINIA

Richmond

Kansas City

St. Louis

Louisville

KENTUCKY

VIRGINIA

MISSOURI

Knoxville

TENNESSEE

APPALACHIAN MTS.

NORTH
CAROLINA

Wilmington

Arkansas R.

Memphis

SOUTH
CAROLINA

Columbia

Little
Rock

Mississippi R.

Atlanta

CAROLINA

Charleston

ARKANSAS

MISSISSIPPI

ALABAMA

GEORGIA

Savannah

orth

LOUISIANA

Vicksburg

Montgomery

Jacksonville

Mobile

New Orleans

Houston

Gulf of Mexico

FLORIDA

N

Robert Louis Stevenson's
route west in 1879 ▰▰▰▰

Map shows major railroads of the United States–1912